FIVE ALIVE

*Revitalize Your Life
One Small Change at a Time*

How Women Can Achieve Success with
Finance, Food, Fitness, Friends, and Fun

JANE MUDGETT

ISBN 978-1-950710-23-2 (Amazon Print)
ISBN 978-1-950710-24-9 (IngramSpark) PAPERBACK
ISBN 978-1-950710-25-6 (Smashwords)

For bulk purchase and for booking, contact:

Jane Mudgett

1646 South Denver Avenue
Tulsa, OK 74119
jane@5-alive.com
jane@janemudgett.com
918-630-8734

I dedicate this book to Love.

ACKNOWLEDGEMENTS

I perceive that some authors get the spark of an idea, a story, and sit down and write a creative fictional piece. Others take their idea and set out for extensive research from an academic perspective. As for me, the seed of this book has been growing for 30 years with many catalysts that you will read about —depression, obesity, the death of my parents, divorce, corporate transfers, extensive work experience in leadership training and development, obtaining my Senior Professional in Human Resources (SPHR) certification as an HR executive, hundreds of employees and coworkers, family members, countless clients, cancer, and nutritional and fitness counseling. These are just the tip of the iceberg of people and experiences that have influenced my current thinking about finance, food, fitness, friends, and fun.

In 2005, I began presenting workshops for women regarding finance and investing. Women often feel shame, guilt, and embarrassment about their lack of knowledge, which means they generally feel more comfortable asking questions within a group of other women. Little do they know that many men are also in the dark about money. What my workshops offered was a safe space to learn and share. Those groups and other seminars, as well as individual client meetings, had the greatest impact on how I think about my values, my path to having more birthdays, my lifestyle, and my desire for longevity. They have provided exceptional examples—like Annette, who was active and sharp until her stroke at 102.5; and the emotionally charged story of a young father who died in his late 40s, leaving two young teenagers and a wife behind to learn to navigate their new life. Your financial advisor may focus only on finances, yet I was lucky that clients included me in many other life decisions.

With this background in mind, I would like to acknowledge some of the positive and strong influencers that contributed to this book directly or indirectly.

I would be foolish not to begin and end with love and gratitude to my husband, Sam Peled. This health journey has been shared for over 28 years. We've experienced many successes and derailments together, including days in hospital recovery rooms and the ICU, and we're stronger and healthier because of it. As I'm writing this, Sam is training for an inline skating marathon in Berlin, and I've crafted a cowbell cheering stick to shake at the finish line. I appreciate his many suggestions and tips, even though he knows I haven't used them all (wink).

My patient and trustworthy writing coach, Wally Schmader, the founder of Exceptional Leaders Lab, not only welcomed me as a partner, but guided me along the way as I tried to share my stories and suggestions throughout this book. His calm and suggestive style worked wonders to guide me toward improvements as he focused on ensuring that I was consistently engaging readers. I feel tremendous gratitude to Wally for his involvement, and he has had a positive impact on my life.

My work partners, Elizabeth Carson, Sanford Roberds, Wilson Fields, and Connie Buckley, have all been so productive, supportive, and patient when I was distracted and disengaged in the financial world because I was working on my community and book activities. My clients and I thank you for your expertise, caring, knowledge, and high level of customer service.

Cece Davis Gifford, RD, CSSD, LD, CLT, and owner of Nutrition Consultants of Tulsa, is my nutritionist, and she has been extremely influential in improving my eating choices and lifestyle. It started with a doctor's order to assist me with low blood sugar and high cholesterol and evolved into a professional and personal relationship over approximately 20 years. Cece turned all of my research—books, articles, and internet mumbo jumbo—into data and facts that I could feel comfortable about not only incorporating into my own eating habits, but also including in the food section of this book. Thank you, Cece. May we be healthy for decades to come.

For the last three years, and maybe the next 30 years give or take, Dani Smith, BS, CPT ACSM, FNS NAM, has used her degree and personal training experience to guide me to better health. Whether my concerns were weight, strength, reducing body fat, increasing muscle mass, or training for ski season or a long bike event, she has demanded and humored me through extensive, varied training at my local YWCA. She has been patient through my aches, arthritis, and pains to focus always on what I can do without shame about what I cannot do. Furthermore, her advice and counsel influence my exercise habits as well as the foods I reach for to feel strong and healthy. Thank you for pushing me and laughing with me at the gym. It's also her voice that resonates in the Food and Fitness sections of the book.

David Brennan from the Human Performance Laboratory at the Center for Exercise and Sports Medicine at the University of Oklahoma (OU) had the biggest impact for my getting off the couch. His presentation at an aging conference at OU included a message that I heard as, "If you're not moving, you're dying." While that may be too direct for some, it was the catalyst I needed. I started my walking program with Katy the next day and haven't stopped moving in one way or another since. He's also great on the keyboard and trumpet and he's a cyclist himself. Thank you, David. You may have no idea of how grateful I am.

My friends and physicians at Hospice of Green Country, Dr. Jeffrey Alderman, Teresa Burkett, JD and RN, Dr. Chandini Sharma, Dr. Jon Cox, and Dr. Jill Wenger, are a few folks with health-care expertise who have shared their knowledge and wisdom over the years. With a specific focus on aging, gerontology, and palliative care, I've learned about my values of living as well as dying, and for this I am eternally grateful. This has served me well via supporting my dad while he received hospice care in Florida to my daily health and wellness decisions. I suspect they will provide "house calls" to me for our future together.

I'm lucky to have my friends who are mental health professionals with expertise in early childhood development to PTSD and other traumas. My thanks go to Elana Newman, Ph.D, for sharing her life experiences with us, including the impactful professional and academic work stories about trauma that she has told us over the decades. The same is true for

Ruth Slocum, LCSW, who introduced me to brain science and feeds my curiosity about brain development. Thanks for helping me process it all over the years. Also, therapist Nelly Vanzetti, Ph.D, has been "on-call" throughout this process to provide details, resources, and references for my many questions regarding human behavior.

There have been hundreds of coworkers, friends, and clients who have been positive—and a few negative—role models for me over the years. I have chosen, for example, not to wait until retirement to work on items on my Life List. Conversely, their social advice influences what restaurants I try, what bike events I register for, what books and articles I read, where I travel in the world, and what I want my lifestyle to be today and into the future. Their comments are woven into my daily activities and, therefore, in this book. The Ski Girls and Ya-Yas are a few of my lifeline calls during life's ups and downs. My chef brother Pete Mudgett has provided cooking advice over the last few years. I now grill more, eat more fish, and use less fat because of his tips and suggestions. My brothers Dave and Pete did not receive culinary skills, nor the developed palate, at our home kitchen table—but we sure know good, healthy food now and have shared some delicious meals over the years.

Life sure is worth living, and it's the people and relationships that make it all worthwhile. We can do our part to extend and enhance our lives through our savings, eating, and movement habits. So much of the world we can't control, but the Five Alive initiative came about because these are some actions we can control if we choose to. To be more alive, I hope you're nudged to make some healthier choices for your own Finance, Food, Fitness, Friends, and Fun.

TABLE OF CONTENTS

LET'S GET STARTED

"The hardest thing in the world is to simplify your life because
everything is pulling you to be more and more complex."
—Yvon Chouinard, the founder of Patagonia

Whatever your age, today is the right day to get started. Today could
be the day you start tackling some of your fears and trepidations.
Today could be the day you take small steps to improve critical and
controllable behaviors in your life that relate to finance, food, fitness,
friends, and fun. This is what I call Five Alive. My premise is twofold.
One, long-term enhancements in our behavior take time and, two, it's
never too late to start.

It's with this mindset that I share this book with you.

After interviews, coaching, training, public speaking, and working
with hundreds of clients, I have learned that at least one of these words—
finance, food, fitness, friends, or fun—is likely to make people (you?)
uncomfortable. It may trigger visceral reactions of negative role models,
guilt, shame, regret, and insecurity. Or, it may generate emotions of
confidence, security, responsibility, and pride. Whatever your reaction,
remember emotions are not reality.

Seeing these reactions in myself and others is what led to researching
the Five Alive topics. I didn't want to share fake claims and fad programs,
so I've sought reliable resources. I've worked hard to ensure advice is
well documented. I've talked with doctors, nutritionists, therapists, and

personal trainers. My information is supported by my own experiences with obesity, depression, low blood sugar, high cholesterol, and cancer.

This book is written in the spirit of no judgment. It's also written with the hope and assumption that you want to improve in at least one of these areas. Furthermore, if you're like most people, you don't want to be told what to do, but you are open to listening to new ideas and suggestions.

I'm asking you to consider making small adjustments every day to create long-term success. *Your* success. Improvements *you* choose—ones that are directly related to your life. And navigating some of these choices and paths may only be easy once they're seen in your rearview mirror.

You'll read the word "nudge" throughout the book. There's quite a bit of research regarding Nudge Theory. You see the word in behavioral science; it relates to small positive reinforcements and indirect suggestions. I've chosen to apply this more broadly to lifestyle ideas that may require a nudge to start small cumulative changes. I call it the "Mudge Nudge."

A Mudge Nudge is a cue, a small stimulus to urge you to pay attention and be mindful of your next step, next choice, or next decision. A nudge is something smaller than a push, more like a tap. You can feel it, but it's not startling or aggressive. A nudge doesn't cause a bruise, just awareness. A nudge may be verbal self-talk, or it may be from your support network. A nudge, in the context of Five Alive, is positive. Here are a few examples of positive nudges.

Finance: You put a sticky note on your credit card that says, "Vacation in Mexico." The note reminds you that you're saving for your next family vacation.

Food: You open the door of your refrigerator or pantry, and the healthy snack choices are at eye level. The less healthy ones are not obvious at first glance. You've created a nudge for yourself to make better choices for your snacks.

Fitness: You get in your car to go to work, and the gym bag is on the passenger seat, packed and ready to go. You've created a visual cue and a reminder that today could be a convenient day to go to the gym.

Friends: In February, you put a reminder in your calendar to look up the spring gardening events and connect with your gardening friends.

Fun: You get online and subscribe to a few local event newsletters so you can start experimenting with new hobbies and activities.

The art of the positive nudge takes practice. We'll try to stay positive in this journey to make small, subtle changes over a long period of time.

Change is woven into the fabric of our heart. Our relationships are dynamic, our bodies may morph, our material needs fluctuate, and our curiosity and interests expand and contract. Over the decades, my body and my life have changed, and things have gotten better, too. In fact, since my 30s, I've made improvements in all of the Five Alive areas, and these improvements have led to greater successes. They've also contributed to me being more open to new experiences, food, people, and movement.

I'm asking you to observe the path you're on and acknowledge that there are variations to the route ahead. There may be a pull created by social media, marketing, and influencers that are difficult to avoid. Yet, there may be a trail that feels better and safer at first glance, even if you don't know why. You may be uncomfortable and a bit anxious about veering off the main path. I'm asking you to trust yourself first, to know what's best for you, to acknowledge the discomfort of these new ideas, as well as the prospect of an enhancement in your life. I suggest that you take more moments here and there to avoid distractions and listen to yourself. Here's a message that has guided me, from Robert Frost's poem, "The Road Not Taken":

> I shall be telling this with a sigh
> Somewhere ages and ages hence:
> Two roads diverged in a wood, and I—
> I took the one less traveled by,
> And that has made all the difference.[1]

As we go, I'm making a few assumptions about you. I assume you'd like to make some adjustments and you're open-minded about a few improvements. I also assume you realize how special you are. You're important to many people around you and in your community. Please take a moment to recognize your own extraordinary value. And, with this recognition of your worth, I hope you desire a full and long life. Even with all of this in place, you may still find that you need a nudge or two along the way.

As we go through these pages together, each section will provide many opportunities to learn about creative ideas and new research, as well as topics that might be familiar to you. There will be something new for everyone to consider as small, positive nudges. Each chapter will include stories and critical information. I'll try to lead you toward the recommendations and then you can narrow them down to the most important takeaways for you.

This is not a "To Do" manual or a "Must Do" requirement; the information shared is for you to strongly consider, adapt, and personalize so you can begin to expand and improve your life, one positive nudge at a time.

The biggest challenge to the Five Alive behaviors is to uncover the tweaks and ideas that are most suitable to you now, and suitable to the person you aspire to be.

We're all affected by Finance, Food, Fitness, Friends, and Fun. You may need or want a change in just one category, or in all five. Go into this process willing to listen. Start from a place where you recognize that these ideas are not criticisms. You're not being judged. Each of us exhibits some behaviors we may wish to adjust and others we want to accept as they are. However, be present and honest with yourself as you think about your lifestyle, your longevity, and the possibilities of living a longer, healthier, fuller, and more active life with few regrets.

By the way, each of the five primary sections—Finance, Food, Fitness, Friends, and Fun—may be read in order or independent of one another. You may choose to read all five sections, or establish priorities depending on the results of your personal assessment.

Below are brief descriptions of the five main sections of the book. At the end of each description, rate your current sense of how you're doing in each Five Alive category using a letter grade of A, B, C, D, or F.

Finance: You know your money behavior when it comes to spending and saving. You save every month for emergencies, retirement, and maybe even your kid's college expenses or a vacation. You have a good idea of how much money you need to pay your bills in full each month.

You and your partner comfortably discuss money issues. You track your income, expenses, savings, and debt.

Your grade: A – B – C – D – F

Food: You eat nutritionally dense foods. You eat very little sugar and do not have a sugar dependency. Your plate includes a variety of colored fruits and vegetables along with grains and lean proteins. You are well hydrated and eat only when you're hungry. You feel good most of the time and think what you eat has a positive impact on your long-term health.

Your grade: A – B – C – D – F

Fitness: You engage in aerobic, strengthening, and flexibility exercises on a regular basis. You try to get in at least 150 minutes (2.5 hours) of exercise each week. You know your stress indicators and have methods for reducing stress. You rarely have aches and pains; you're not deterred, and you keep moving. You include activities that stimulate your brain as well as your body.

Your grade: A – B – C – D – F

Friends: You have meaningful relationships in your life, which may or may not include a life partner. You have friends and family in your life who provide social and emotional support. You have a few close friends with whom you share your joys and disappointments. You do not feel lonely most of the time. You're open to meeting new people in your community. You believe having friends is important.

Your grade: A – B – C – D – F

Fun: You know what fun means to you and what makes you smile. Sometimes you lose track of time when you're involved with your personal interests. You're willing to try new things to find additional activities that capture your attention. You're open to meeting new people with similar interests.

Your grade: A – B – C – D – F

Now that you've graded yourself, I recommend that you read the five main sections of the book in order of their grade, from the best grade to the worst. This strategy will feel comfortable as you will relate more to the initial sections you read. You may identify a few new ideas to incorporate into the way you live your life now. As you progress, you may find areas that are a bit more challenging and places where you need to linger and reflect before you establish new goals and intentions.

In each section, I'll include a few Secrets, Hacks, and Mudge Nudges to keep you going. At the end of each section, I'll provide a chapter summary as a quick reference and then I'll give you a chance to grade yourself again, create some personal goals, and come up with a few of your own positive nudges. How does that sound?

OK, now one more Mudge Nudge – we're taking the road less traveled.

SECTION I

FINANCE

"Money is only a tool. It will take you wherever you wish,
but it will not replace you as the driver."
—Ayn Rand

1

HOW I LEARNED MY MONEY MESSAGES

Like so many events that happen in our lives, sometimes jobs are planned, sometimes they're luck, and sometimes we stumble into opportunities. For me, the evolution of my career was a combination of all three—planning, luck, and stumbling. Over the next several pages, I'll describe my relationship with money and finance. This context will help you understand why I'm passionate about helping women improve their knowledge of, and relationship to, money and I'll also lay the groundwork for what we'll work on together in this chapter.

At 20, I graduated from Florida State University with a business degree—the degree I had wanted since I was 13. That's when my dad told me a story about an economics for the final exam, the professor had simply written a statement on the chalkboard, "Explain the law of supply and demand. You have two hours." My dad ferociously wrote the entire time, with comments about money supply, manufacturing, consumer demand, and how supply and demand create equilibrium pricing. Needless to say, he had become an expert, shared much of what he learned with me and I walked away from his story with a decent business lesson at a young age. I was intrigued.

At 15, I asked my parents' permission to get a job so I could earn my own money, but they didn't think it was a good idea. They said I had my whole life to work, but since I was adamant, they suggested I wait a year until I didn't need their permission. Well, I waited precisely one year and then got a job in a clothing store in Daytona Beach. After my first few paychecks, I opened a checking and a savings account. My father taught me to deposit some money into my savings account every time I made a deposit to checking and to balance my checkbook by using the template on the back of the monthly statements. (I still do this today, but online.)

The following year, I needed $2,000 to buy a car for driving to school and work. The deal was that my folks would pay for insurance if I bought the car. I still remember my pride when I made the deposit that brought my bank balance over $2,000. I then asked for a cashier's check for $2,000 to pay my parents for the car they'd arranged to buy for me. I also remember my shock and frustration when the teller said the check had to clear before I could make a withdrawal. WHAT? I had planned to the penny to have the right amount of funds available. My dad was going to pick up the car soon. He had to have the money to buy the car. A bank policy that I had no idea about was between me and my major transaction. How come no one told me this?!

I paced the lobby a bit and finally remembered that our neighbor worked in the bank. My memory is that I demanded to see him and sought his help. I had no idea what miracle was needed to get the $2,000 check. But, I walked out of there full of pride and confidence—and with a $2,000 check in my hand, made out to my parents so they could buy my used red Toyota Corolla.

A year later, my father helped me get a small loan at the bank. I didn't need to borrow money, but he wanted me to start building my credit. Once again, I was clueless. "Why?" I asked. A family friend had recently been turned down for a mortgage. It made no sense. He was 40ish, educated, had worked for 20 years, and paid his bills on time, but had no credit history. My father was getting ahead of that game with me. He had me borrow $1,000, and I paid it back before I finished high school.

Finance Secret: Parents and other influential people in our lives teach us indirect and direct lessons about spending and saving. These are called "money messages." Everyone has learned them, and you may even be passing some along, too.

Take a moment to think about the people who have influenced how you feel about money. Some of us take money for granted. Some of us overspend. Some of us hoard savings. Your money lessons may not have been formed by your parents; they may have come from other family members or friends, but all of us have been influenced by the culture and society at the time of our upbringing.

After high school, between work and scholarships, I headed to Florida State University and earned that business degree I had my eye on since 13. So, you now have a picture of some of the money messages I learned growing up. However, you only know one part of the picture of influence. Did my mother share my father's money behavior? No way!

While my father, the last of seven children, was brought up poor during the Depression, my mother, an only child, was brought up with a very different experience during the same time period. I heard stories of being poor from my father, but these weren't echoed by my mother. There were pockets where people didn't feel the Depression and appeared not to sacrifice as others had. I have come to believe this is the case with the maternal side of my family.

Driven by fear of poverty, my father worked obsessively. That included traveling out of town and out of the country. My mother was left to care for the kids and the household. My mom, from her upbringing, was accustomed to buying all of what she needed as well as most of what she wanted. This thinking didn't change after serving in the Navy and after marriage. This behavior, I believe, made the gerbil—my father—run even faster on the wheel to generate income.

What I eventually learned was that a portion of my mom's spending was more emotional than practical. I could relate this behavior to my emotional overeating. When emotions manifest in money, there may be a foundation of insecurity, depression, or loneliness that lead to "retail therapy." I never got to have this discussion with my mother, but I suspect she hadn't planned on having that many days and weeks parenting alone. Suffice it to say, I learned that buying things was an acceptable way of self-medicating to change one's mood.

I also know that overspending is much more complicated than I've outlined. If you can identify with this, I highly recommend that you invest time to uncover the root of this behavior. It means tracking your expenses with your emotions at the time of spending. Think about the money lessons you learned growing up, particularly in your pre-teen and teenage years. It could be that you purchase more when you're upset or feel the need to reward yourself. We'll talk more about this later, but take a moment now to think about your own habits.

During college, I was a miser and kept track of my income, scholarships, and expenses on a green accounting ledger sheet (I realize everything is online now). After college, starting a professional career, and getting married, I kept this same system even when expenses became a bit more complicated. In later years, I moved this manual system to Quicken software, so I could develop reports easily from the data I was collecting.

This system worked well for years. As the primary breadwinner, I felt good about our finances. It worked so well that when my then-husband wanted to take over the bill paying, I thought it would be a piece of cake. I showed him how to use Quicken to record our checks, credit card expenditures, and income. Simultaneously, we were having some marital challenges, and I was home alone one day contemplating divorce. I realized we needed to have our finances in order before anything else. I checked out our Quicken account on the computer and was shocked. He had been paying the minimum amounts on the credit card bills instead of the full balance each month. We had both the money to pay the bills and the wherewithal to stop spending. How could this have happened? I was devastated. There would be no divorce anytime soon. I had to put together a plan to stop the financial bleeding, pay off credit cards, and get our savings back in order.

I took over the checkbook again and started to hoard cash. We did not go out. Our discretionary spending was brought to a minimum. Holiday gifts were either tiny or consisted of a donation to honor a friend or family member. I made large payments to credit cards and reduced our debt by thousands of dollars.

As a professional woman traveling alone, I frequently had dinner with my business associates and would then return to my hotel. One night alone in a Los Angeles hotel I concluded, "I can be *at least* this happy all by myself." This realization eventually led to my divorce.

I started my new life with one income, a home and mortgage, my name on someone else's car loan, and over $15,000 of credit card debt. I was turned down for my own credit card because my debt to income ratio didn't meet the requirements. The reality was that I had a company car, half a mortgage, and half the credit card debt, but these were different times for women and credit. The marriage may not have been saved, but financially, this was a tough blow.

Those are a few of my formative stories about money. Maybe this has triggered a few of your own money memories. Think about your early spending and savings lessons and experiences. Were they generally positive? For some of us, money is simple and for others, money seems complicated. I hope you find that there doesn't have to be a mystique about money and finances.

Let's take some of the concepts I've shared and break them down to apply to your life.

2

SAVE FIRST AND THEN SPEND

Let's start with a comment that is not uncommon in the world of financial planning, "I'd like to have enough money not to worry—you know, be rich." It seems so easy to say, but to the listener, it means nothing. What is rich? What does rich mean to you?

- Having $1,000,000 in the bank? _____

- Enough money for you, your kids, and your grandchildren? _____

- Having no debt and being able to buy what you want? _____

- Owning an expensive home or a second home on the beach? _____

- How will you know when you're rich? _____

One of the wealthiest men in the United States, Warren Buffet lives in a regular house and drives a regular car and lives in Omaha. I drove by his suburban home once. It's not bad—pleasant, nice lawn, but nothing special. There was no apparent extra security or paparazzi circling the perimeter when I drove by.

So, how will you get to this land of richness and how will you know when you get there? As the phrase goes, "If you don't know where you're going, any road will take you there ... it doesn't matter which way you go."

> *"The biggest barrier to becoming rich is living*
> *like you're rich before you are."*[2]
>
> —Knight Kiplinger

I had an acquaintance who thought he would be inheriting money when his stepmother died. The stepmother was my client, and I was not allowed to share any details about the beneficiaries or the estate. In anticipation, he went out and bought a brand-new car, which he couldn't afford with his current income. It was OK because the inheritance was coming soon, right? Well, you already know where this story is going. He didn't receive the inheritance. He did, however, create some real financial issues because he counted the chickens before they hatched. I also observed this when I worked in human resources in a couple of large corporations. Before bonus time, some folks started spending money they hadn't received yet. However, in real life it's more common that smaller expenditures add up quickly—going out to eat more, hiring a cleaning service for your home, expanding your gym membership to include a personal trainer, setting automatic payments for online services, or buying more new clothes. When I've analyzed expenses, including my own, it's often spending of less than $100 that adds up quickly. In other words, a lower amount of dollars, but a higher frequency of spending.

Mudge Nudge: Pay yourself first. Contribute to savings before you start paying your bills. And never stop saving. If times get lean, reduce the amount you save, but don't stop all together.

When you're in the financial industry, like I was, you realize you can't jump to conclusions. You may think someone is wealthy, when in reality, they merely have good taste in clothing and cars. Or, they may be the millionaire driving a 10-year-old Toyota Camry. Or, they may be the farmer in Georgia who was referred to the Cadillac dealer because the Lincoln dealer didn't think he could afford a Lincoln. Well, he liked the Cadillac he bought for his wife so much, he bought one for himself too—and paid cash for both! Generally, however, it's the "invisible rich," millionaire next door, the guy in a ball cap, or the woman driving a compact car who may surprise you. Here are some of the common money traits we observe in the invisible rich:

- Spend less than they earn
- Pay themselves first; deposit into savings before checking
- Money they don't see, they don't spend
- Sock away raises and bonuses rather than flaunting them
- Learn to say "no," "maybe later," or "not now" to salespeople

Is this what you observe in your family, friends, or in social networks? Ask yourself:

- Do your friends influence what you spend money on?
- What are the money messages you're observing?
- What about a person makes you think they're wealthy?
- What did you learn about money when you were growing up?

Your social network may have a positive influence on how much you save, or it may be making you broke. Are your friends going to the big-name concerts? You going along, too? Do they recommend a casual restaurant or the three-star Michelin location? I can hear my friend say, "When was the last time you did something nice for yourself? Come on, you can afford it." In reality, they don't know what I can or cannot afford.

Mudge Nudge: Be creative when reducing expenses—get together with friends with a take-out dinner from a restaurant and enjoy it at home. You'll save money on the tip, and alcohol at home is much less expensive.

Social media may also be making you broke. Facebook, Twitter, Instagram, and Pinterest (or the NEXT social media) **are** influencing your spending decisions. They promote more impulse buying based on how people dress, where they vacation, what their new furniture looks like. They use videos, beautiful photos, and lovely colors to capture your attention. Companies install cookies on your computer so the products you search for keep appearing so you can see their beauty and value. You may not even notice the ads between the posts of your friends or along the side bars. The ad may be "liked" by a friend, so of course you look at it. It's a visual buffet of material goods that the marketing world believes you need and want. It appears to be an all-you-can-eat smorgasbord where you'll never gain weight, "But wait, there's more!" You may tag items and create wish lists. You may put an item in the online shopping cart, decide not to buy it, and close out of the internet. The next time you go online, the company has emailed you … How did they find you? Jeez, you gave them your email to get the extra 15% off. Do you ever feel like you're being stalked online? I do.

Invest a few minutes to note how your social groups and social media are impacting your spending. Think about how your family and friends influence your spending. It's not necessarily good nor bad; but it's worth noticing.

There's no way around it: our spending habits are influenced by others. We're all predisposed to certain situations such as our gender, culture, demographics, and religious beliefs. Knowing this can help us be more aware and deliberate in our choices.

In addition, trends change at a much quicker pace, and it costs money to stay ahead or catch up with the trends. The Census Bureau and the Bureau of Labor Statistics illustrate this with some of their research, some of which may surprise you:

- Women are delaying marriage, and divorce rates for women over 55 are increasing, creating an increasing percentage of single working-age women in our economy.
- Women are obtaining more bachelor's degrees than men, and they are having fewer children.
- Women are the primary breadwinners for nearly 30% of households, and they are co-breadwinners slightly more than 50% of the time.

- Homeownership rates are now equal for men and women at 50% for each gender.

According to the Center for American Progress, women contribute over *$7 trillion* to the U.S. GDP each year. And, our spending is influenced by those we are surrounded by, but particularly by women.

Here's an illustration of my comments. My brother is successful. He has a degree in business and urban planning and got involved with commercial real estate development soon after graduate school. One of his college buddies was also on a successful career trajectory. His friend was smart and moving up the corporate ladder quickly, and my brother perceived (or knew) that he was behind him financially. When his friend became the youngest treasurer of a multinational energy company, my brother knew he could not only <u>not</u> keep up, but he couldn't compete with "keeping up with the Joneses." Sometimes, we must appreciate our friends as just that: friends and <u>not</u> financial competitors.

Mudge Nudge: The more money you have, the more there is to manage. Said another way, it's easier to budget when you don't have much money. To keep up as you add wealth, shift from dollar amounts and simple cash flow to expense ratios as a percentage of your income.

After visiting 36 countries (and counting), I believe that Americans are some of the best marketers in the world. Thanks to early lessons from Dale Carnegie in the 1920s and Madison Avenue in the 1950s and 1960s, we know how to influence people to buy stuff. Our economy is based on consumer consumption; that is, it depends on us spending money. If the invisible hand that economist Adam Smith referred to had its way, the hand would reach right into our pockets and we would spend more than we earn … for the betterment of the country. All of this is strengthened or exacerbated by easy-to-obtain loans and credit cards.

The author and wealth psychology expert and financial advisor, Kathleen Burns Kingsbury, notes that many of our money messages are learned from others before we're 12 or 13. Were you rewarded for buying nice things with your allowance or rewarded for saving, is one example she might cite. What did you observe from close friends and family while growing up?

Analyze your relationship with money and ask:

- What is your temperament when you think of money?
- Who influenced the way you think about money?
- Do you spend a lot, and do you know why?
- Do you save up to the point of oversimplifying your lifestyle?
- How does money impact your marriage and other relationships?

We think about needs versus wants, but another approach is to compare if an item is needed versus *deserved*. This is a different approach to connect emotions with spending. Using the language "deserved" adds an element of reward or an opportunity to even a score for a negative event. Maybe you can relate to this: "I had such a tough day at work. We could barely break for lunch. I think I'll stop by the Nordstrom's sale on the way home. I deserve something special after what I've been through."

Investing time to better understanding your money personality, even if it includes counseling or therapy, could be worthwhile. For many people, talking about money is more personal, more sensitive, more confidential, than talking about most other intimate details about their lives.

Here's an example. I was having coffee with a female friend, talking about this book and other ideas. To illustrate the point above, I asked a number of questions regarding the sex life of her friends. Is the sex good? Do they complain about it? Is it enough? Is it frequent? These were very personal questions, but she knew the answers for most of her friends. I said, Okay, now what do you know about their income? How much debt do they have? Do they have emergency savings? And I asked other money-related questions about her circle of friends. She shrugged and admitted she didn't know any of the answers.

A frequent reason you hear for divorce is how one spouse handled money. Many couples not only don't talk about money before they're married, but they have minimal conversations about it *after* marriage (or making a long-term commitment). Well, all I can say is that I hope the sex is good!

It's also important to discuss your habits and values related to making and spending money.

3

YOUR TWO-PURPOSE PAYCHECK—TODAY AND THE FUTURE

In the following sections, we're going to go deep on money and your relationship with it. In certain sections, you may feel like you're doing a bad job. This is true for all of us. There's a lot of shame associated with spending and money management. This is a no-judgment, guilt-free zone. We're going to talk honestly about spending, help you understand where you have room for improvement, and then make some recommendations that will help you enhance your situation.

So, let's get it out there. Where do you spend money now? Are you keeping any kind of records with your bank, credit cards, or online shopping to determine where your paycheck is spent? To do that, try this task:

- Identify everywhere that you consistently spend money each month.

- Separate out the fixed costs. A fixed cost would continue even if you lost your job. It includes items such as rent, mortgage, utilities, groceries, and car payments. These are the things you *need*.

- Identify all your discretionary or variable costs. These items may vary based on how much you get paid. These include electronic gadgets, special TV cable or streaming products, eating out, sports, hobbies, concerts. These items vary by the amount of money you make and could go away if you lose your job. Generally, these are the things you *want*.

Now that you have these items identified, calculate how much you spend on fixed and discretionary expenses. Compare this to your paycheck to determine how much is left for savings.

The first goal is to be cautious when you add or increase a fixed cost. The second goal is to keep your fixed costs *low* as a *percentage* of your total income. This will enhance your feeling of security, especially when it's combined with retirement and both short-term and long-term savings. By having lower fixed costs, it will be easier to increase savings or handle unexpected expenses.

In 2008–2009, the stock market was dropping until it finally hit bottom on March 9, 2009. I was in the financial services industry; this was how I earned a living. Suddenly, people's net worth dropped dramatically, and it took years to regain lost ground. What we learned was that the folks with conservative and/or well-balanced portfolios did better. The people with savings to ride out the downturn did fine. Those who had both of these *and* low fixed costs, not only survived but were comfortable, even in a period of financial market chaos. It was part patience, part good planning, and part ability to spend less when needed.

In addition to using online budgeting, you may adjust your automatic bill-paying process. You can set up a system as a push, sending money from your account to a vendor, or a **pull**, when the vendors access your account and take the funds they need to pay the current bill. I'm an advocate for the **push** system for paying bills. However, consider the **pull** system for automatic savings so you can pay yourself first. While it's less convenient, you could pay your fixed costs like your mortgage and utility payments automatically when they're received. However, set up a manual process for your other discretionary expenses that have varying balances. This forces you to review these bills before paying them. Be careful of automatic payment schedules. I have reviewed many budgets with clients who cannot identify recurring charges. They may have been paying for services they haven't used for many months, or years.

Designate where to **push** money from your account to:

_____

_____

Designate where to **pull** money into your account from:

_____

_____

Hack: The people who save more are those who directly deposit funds from their paycheck into savings accounts and subscribe to the "pay yourself first" approach. The funds that are remaining are used to pay bills. Therefore, the reverse is also true. Folks who pay bills first and then save, generally save less.

Your discretionary costs should fluctuate based on your income; that is, the more you make, the more dollars you may spend or save (the percentages may remain about the same). The goal is to plan, organize, and control your discretionary spending. However, as your wealth increases, you may notice how many more items become fixed or discretionary. The more you know about your own spending habits, the better you can make adjustments over time, such as when that new baby arrives and when a new car is needed — which may go with the new baby!

Mudge Nudge: Don't forget to keep up with compensation data for your professional roles and responsibilities. Follow up if adjustments are needed to reach parity and best practices in your industry. As of now, men are more likely to ask for raises than women. We need to catch up with this trend!

Too much discretionary spending early crowds out future savings, investments, and your future lifestyle. This is a good illustration of how the "pay yourself first" approach works for savings. Also, your paycheck today has at least two purposes: the money you need now and the money you'll need during retirement. This means your spending behavior today *will* impact your lifestyle of tomorrow. Think about it.

> Today's paycheck = Today's lifestyle and expenses +
> Retirement lifestyle and expenses

Couples who combine their paychecks into joint checking and savings accounts save more in the long run. When the checking account balance gets too high, automatically move money into savings. It's easier for us to make this decision with a partner. Openly discuss the advantages and disadvantages of having separate or joint accounts. If you don't care to combine your paychecks, then allocate a portion of your paycheck to a household account to pay the joint bills. Together discuss what percentage each of you will contribute to the household savings and checking accounts to pay the bills. Base this on how much each of you contribute to your joint income. If your pay is not equal, do not put the same percentage of your paycheck into the joint household account. Here's an example:

> Partner A makes $60,000 per year, $5,000 per month
>
> Partner B makes $90,000 per year, $7,500 per month
>
> Together, they make $150,000, $12,500 per month
>
> Partner A makes 40% of the total, and Partner B makes 60% of the total.
>
> They need $10,000 per month in their household account for expenses, therefore
>
> Partner A contributes $4,000 per month (40% of $10,000), and
>
> Partner B contributes $6,000 per month (60% of $10,000).

With this simple equation, this couple has $2,500 left over for savings per month. This should be directed to emergency savings, retirement, college, travel, and miscellaneous savings. (By the way, when you learn to pay yourself first through savings, the advanced version is to calculate the amount that each partner contributes *after* you put aside your savings. Some people call this, "Pay yourself first.")

If you generally pay with a credit card, review *every* line of these statements *every* month. You will be amazed how many errors you will find. I have been charged for items I never purchased, but I have also not been charged for items I have purchased. Keep receipts on product returns until you see a credit on your statement, because sometimes your transactions get overlooked.

Now that I've remarried, my husband and I each use Quicken. Are we nerds or what?! He puts in every expense from our credit card statements every month and all our other bills, too. This allows us to better analyze our expenses. Many banks and investment companies offer this and there are dozens of budgeting apps used by millions of people who can do the same type of recording, aggregation, and budget reporting. For security purposes, we choose not to use apps that link to our bank accounts. We also save our information on a hard drive, not in the cloud. OK, we're dinosaurs, I admit it. However, if you're only using the app to plug in your numbers this may be easier than making a spreadsheet from scratch. Many people want me and other financial advisors to recommend apps, but I am choosing not to. Some apps use your data, some sell it. Varying degrees of cybersecurity exist; some are simple, others are robust. I know plenty of people who use and love them, but I'm staying out of this one.

Once per year, review every bill you pay during the month. Identify any items that you may shop around for or can negotiate. Many people are successful at reducing interest rates on their credit cards, monthly cable/movie/streaming bills, internet, insurance, and negotiating better phone rates. Be sure to shop for insurance every two to three years. There may be a discount in your future. Furthermore, try not to let marketing schemes and current social trends influence your decisions if they're not in sync with your financial goals.

4

WHAT'S COMING IN AND WHAT'S GOING OUT

Now, go back to look around at your friends, family, and other people in your life. Identify those you admire as positive financial role models. (Yes, it may be your *perception* of their money skills). Seek them out and ask them if they could share some of their financial experiences with you. What were their money messages growing up? Will they share their lessons with you? Here are a few ideas of potential role models:

- Recent immigrants—many of whom saved to come here. In addition, they may not have credit established yet, so they make purchases with cash and with savings.

- The millionaire next door—do you know anyone like this?

- Early retirees—how did they accomplish this goal?

- Parents and grandparents—do they have lifestyles that you admire? How do they accomplish this?

If you have these role models in your life, ask them about their stories of success. They don't have to include personal financial details for you to glean a few pearls and ideas for your own life. For instance, maybe they shared family dinners to save money. Some people pool resources for joint ownership of a home or vehicle. Others pay cash for everything instead of using credit cards to help control their spending. It may be fascinating to hear about their financial challenges and how they overcame them.

Finance Secret: Positive financial role models, like the ones above, know what money is coming in, what money is going out, what money is going to short-term and long-term savings, and what needs to be invested. And if they don't have that information at their fingertips, they know where to find it quickly.

5

START SAVING NOW AND NEVER STOP

We've talked quite a bit about tracking and managing expenses, but we still need to address non-retirement savings. In 1960, families in the United States saved about 10% of their income. In 2017, that number was closer to 2.5%. The countries with the highest savings rates were Switzerland, Luxembourg, Sweden, Germany, and Hungary. The United States was not in the top or bottom percentile for non-retirement savings.

Let's start with your personal situation. What's your single or joint income? What percentage do you save? Financial celebrities scream at us to save more, and there's a part of me that strongly agrees. I just don't like to yell. "Dave R." says start with a small balance of $1,000 in savings and after debt is paid off, increase savings to cover one month and then six months of living expenses. (I have different ideas about debt. Stay tuned!) "Suze" says one to six months of living expenses in savings is common, but she recommends 8–12 months in emergency savings.

If your balance today is $0, set up direct deposit and begin contributing to an emergency savings account *now*. I'm serious. When things go downhill, it's a slippery slope of losing jobs, car maintenance, kids' expenses, health care, and who knows what else. *Anything* beats $0. Start today. Put this book down and do this right now. I'm not kidding.

Savings may be harder when the amount you're able to save is low. It's easy to brush it off as insignificant. However, if you can build your savings muscles when the dollar or the percentage of your pay amounts are low, they will be there when you begin to earn more money. You'll then see the advantages of the habit pay off through compounding interest and larger balances.

When your balance gets to $1,000, keep going based on what your real monthly living expenses are. Yes, you do need *months* of expenses in a savings account. Try to put it in a money market account to get some interest paid on it. Don't put it under the mattress, because you will spend cash. Deposit it in a bank so it's federally insured (FDIC).

Calculate how much you need for your monthly bills and then calculate your savings goal. Start by saving $1,000 and then keep going.

- Emergency savings goal of 1 month = $_____
- Emergency savings goal of 3 months = $ _____
- Emergency savings goal of 6 months = $ _____

When I was about 21, I went to a women's conference. There were women presenting ideas about leadership, there was a fashion show for new looks for professional women, and there was a financial speaker, Mara Levitt. Mara talked about savings and investing (including emergency savings) and she put me on the right track. I got her card and saved it for four or five years. When I had saved $5,000 over and above everything else I needed, I went to see Mara at a stockbroker's office. I wanted advice for my big investment. To her credit, she did not mock or laugh, she praised me. She encouraged me to save more. I did, and I took her advice for about 10 years before I moved to a state where she was not licensed. I have valued the advice of financial professionals since I was 25. Obviously, I am grateful because I can still remember her name. Thank you, Mara.

6

SAVING TODAY FOR TOMORROW

Your Retirement Savings. What about it?

Today's paycheck = Today's expenses and lifestyle +
Retirement expenses and lifestyle

If your company has a retirement savings plan such as a 401(k) or a 403(b), sign up for it and start making deposits via payroll deductions. Today. No kidding. Unless you plan on working until you die, or you're confident that there will be Social Security and you can live on Social Security alone, save for retirement. No one else is doing this for you. Be your own savings advocate.

If the company matches a specific percentage of your pay, put that amount in, or more. If the company match is 4%, you are *not* **maxing out** when you contribute 4% of your salary. You're receiving the maximum match from your company. You **max out** when you hit the federal cap, which is about $19,500 per year (2020). Be sure to get the up-to-date dollar cap because this number changes annually. When you contribute $19,500 from your pay to your 401(k)/403(b), you will then **max out** what you can contribute—and not one dollar before that cap. As a financial advisor, people told me all the time they were maxing out their 401(k), and more often than not, they were *not*. In order to maximize your retirement savings, it's important to understand this distinction.

Two additional thoughts about common retirement plans—the simple version:

1) Contributing to a 401(k), 403(b), or an IRA are all winners because you win on taxes whether your investment does anything or not. You reduce your income taxes when you make the contributions, so you're well ahead simply by protecting those funds. You also don't pay taxes when the investments increase and grow. You will, however, pay income taxes when you begin to take withdrawals, such as at retirement.

2) An alternative is to contribute to a Roth 401(k) if your employer has this option available to you. Although you will not receive a tax benefit when you make contributions, you will still have two long-term tax benefits. A) You won't pay taxes when the investments increase and grow. B) Different from the traditional 401(k), you will *not* have to pay taxes when you begin taking withdrawals, such as at retirement. Many people overlook this option, but it's worth investigating. If you have a tax preparer, ask them for an opinion about whether the tax laws are the same and whether a Roth IRA is right for you.

Because I'm a numbers and a financial person, I'm champing at the bit to share all sorts of examples and calculations with you. Only about 1% of you will appreciate it, but allow me to share one example about how investments can increase anyway.

Example: If you contribute $1,500 per month for 10 years, and the market improves by 6% per year, your balance will grow to about $250,000. You'll have a quarter of a million bucks!

Finance Secret: The federal government dictates what percentage of your pay or dollar amount you can contribute to your retirement plan. It does not limit the amount an employer can contribute on your behalf, but the employer generally has a limit. Check out what the limit is; it's usually expressed as a percentage of your salary. I have seen matches of 0%–12% ... and if it's above 1%, get that match into your retirement account. Start today. No kidding.

The best way to build your retirement account balance is to continually contribute each month over all your working years. These funds must then be invested to grow. (Check out www.investor.gov.) Arrange for investing all your contributions as well as the company match. Also, get online to set up automatic increases of your contributions each year. If you receive raises and bonuses, add these to your retirement account balance. You've already been living on less income, so you won't notice the difference day to day, but your savings will balloon. And the younger you are, the more it grows. Or, said another way, the longer you make deposits and contributions, the higher the account balance will be in the future. Use apps or online retirement calculators and consult your retirement plan representative or your financial advisor to develop a long-range savings plan. Invest in target-retirement-date mutual funds or ask your advisor for recommendations. Remember your paycheck and total income has **two** purposes.

Today's paycheck = Today's lifestyle and expenses +
Retirement lifestyle and expenses

The prior example about contributing to a retirement plan illustrates how money grows over time when it's invested in the stock market. It grows by gaining value based on what you contribute and on the growth of the stock market. Savings accounts also grow, but not based on the stock market activity. Savings accounts grow based on the interest rate the bank pays you for storing your money there. Banks use your money to lend to others, and they pay you interest in return.

A professional woman came in to visit me after attending a workshop. She had a good income and was a good saver. She felt that she was out of control, however, because she had five different 401(k)s, four from prior employers. She was barely paying attention to her current plan and was ignoring the other plans. She had some account statements, but not all were current. What should she do?

She should obtain current statements from all retirement accounts. She should consider consolidating (rollover from 401(k) to an IRA) all the accounts into one Individual Retirement Account (IRA). The next step is to work with her financial advisor to develop an investment plan that corresponds to her lifestyle goals. Finally, she should also discuss her current employer's retirement plan to ensure its investments are in sync with her IRA investments.

Over time, as you save in company retirement plans and change jobs, your IRA will become one of your largest assets. It will be the main repository of your retirement savings.

I know many combinations and permutations of what you can do with your retirement plans. Focus on contributions, not borrowing, and not making withdrawals. If you have to reduce the amount you contribute, go ahead. But don't stop contributing. Put a note in your calendar to remind yourself to try to increase your contributions later or set up the automatic increases. No one else is making deposits for you.

It is *not* too late to begin contributing into your employer-sponsored retirement plan. Just do it. Start today. Increase the amount you contribute over time, and later you'll be grateful you have these funds. They may be used for health care, living expenses, or buying a fancy car. You won't know until you get there—maybe decades from now.

A note about non-retirement assets and women:

If you've paid your bills and fulfilled all of your savings requirements and there's money left over, open a non-retirement general investment account. Women control 19% of all investable assets in the United States—as decision makers, not just influencers. Women control approximately 10% of all private wealth, and that number is expected to rise. According to the Boston Consulting Group, from 2010 to 2015, the amount of private wealth that women controlled increased by 50%, which equates to $72 trillion dollars by 2020. Because women have a longer lifespan than men, those numbers are expected to rise as more wealth moves into their hands. You don't have to be an expert investor. Use your expertise to find someone you trust with experience and credentials. Work collaboratively to fulfill your financial goals.

Mudge Nudge: Invest a bit more assertively or pay the price. Women are generally more conservative investors. If that describes you, you may need to increase the amount you save and invest to make up for a more conservative philosophy. Be sure to discuss this with your investment advisor and include this premise in your financial plan.

Final comments about savings …

You may always be juggling what you save and when you save depending on your needs, values, and wants. This is life and nothing is fixed and set in stone. You may need a new car, a big vacation may be in your future, your child may decide they're not ready for college after you've saved for it, the air conditioning unit might go out, you want a new carbon-fiber bike, your grandmother needs help for health-care deductibles, your pet requires treatment … that's OK, that's life. Make it a good one. Yes, make a plan and start saving for what's important in your life and juggle some funds around. Accept the fact that all plans should be written in pencil, erased, and edited many times in one's life. It's OK. Breath. Give yourself credit for what you're doing well. And, don't forget to pay yourself first. You're worth it!

7

BUDGET—THE OTHER B WORD

The best way to reduce debt is to not accrue it in the first place. If you have a spending and savings plan, sometimes called a budget (the other B word), then you may not need to borrow. The reality is that most of us will need to borrow for big purchases such as a house or car. So, let's spend some time on this, and then other types of debt.

Let's start with your goal to buy a car, the most common type of loan. Do not let the bank, the dealership, or the car lot determine how much you can afford to spend. Only you should know what your true income and expenses are and, therefore, what monthly payment you can afford. Generally, they will try to persuade you to spend much more than you need to spend at higher interest rates and for longer periods of time. Do you really want a $60,000 truck, at 5% interest for 72 months? (You'll pay about $10,000 in interest for this over and above the price of the truck.) The goal of the business and of capitalism is to make as much money as possible ... and that means the money must come from me and you. So remember, *you* are your own best financial advocate.

Go back to your budget (oops, I said it) and look at your income, expenses, and savings and determine what you can afford for a monthly payment. Try to obtain the lowest interest rate possible. Zero to 3% is not uncommon for new cars; used cars generally have slightly higher interest rates. Use an online calculator to determine *in advance* how much you're willing to spend and a range of monthly payments based on common interest rates and your budget. They want to <u>sell</u> you a car, but I'm suggesting that, instead, you control <u>buying</u> the car. Do your homework before selecting and test-driving cars. Once you get into the vehicles, it's hard to turn back. Once you drive them, it gets even harder. And, if you're also smelling that new car smell, well, you get the message. Bottom line: know what your acceptable monthly payment is before you test-drive anything.

For many of us, the largest purchase in our lifetime is our home. The same rules for purchasing a car remain true for this purchase. Determine in advance what you can afford. The bank, realtor, and mortgage companies will pre-approve us for a home much more expensive than most of us need. A good rule of thumb is that your home payments should be between 25% and 35% of your gross income.

Home payments include all of these costs:

1. Mortgage (principal and interest) +

2. Homeowners' and possibly mortgage insurance +

3. Property taxes +

4. Condo and Association fees +

Let's say you make $ _____. I'll start at $100,000 gross income per year. Therefore, *total* home expense range could be $25,000–$35,000 per year or $2,081–$2,916 per month. However, the details make all the difference in the world, so be sure to get approximate tax rates and insurance rates for your calculation.

What's the significant missing element above? Your down payment. The more you save to use as a down payment, the **lower your monthly payments**. If you have a greater down payment, you may not be required to pay for PMI (private mortgage insurance). The larger your down payment, the lower your interest rate will be. Why? The more money you put down tells the lender that you are a lower risk because you have responsibly saved money for the purpose of buying a home. They'll also review your credit score, so get that in advance. (Go to annualcreditreport.com.) A lower interest rate reduces the total amount of interest you'll pay (even if it is currently tax-deductible). In addition, you have a higher personal investment in the house. Remember, you must also have funds for closing costs, home repairs, and decorating your new home. This is not what emergency savings should be used for.

I've heard from friends that their goal was to buy the least expensive home in an expensive neighborhood. This approach is logical for resale and for a home to hold its value. Thomas J. Stanley, the author of *Stop Acting Rich*, said "one's home or neighborhood is their greatest detriment to building wealth ... If you live in a pricey home and neighborhood, you will act and buy like your neighbors ... we take our consumption cues from our neighbors." I know I've done this in the past and it's a powerful force. This is another subtle example of how neighbors will spend your money.

The elephant in the room is the greatest debt risk of all: credit cards. Credit card companies want you to spend as much money as possible on their card. They persuade you to use their cards with cash back, airline miles, and award points. They want you to pay the minimum balance so they will have interest payments from you for as long as possible. They make money from the annual fees, sure. But the big profit is made when you don't pay your balance in full every month. Some of this profit is used to provide cash back, airline miles, and award points. See the connection?

Your goal for your credit cards is to use them for a temporary loan during the month as you buy things. When the statement arrives, you silently thank them for helping you with the monthly cash flow and you pay the bill *in full* each and every month. You will feel more comfortable not carrying a bunch of cash around in your wallet. It's as simple as that. Period. Other than loan sharks, the highest interest rates out there today are on unpaid balances of credit cards. It's the opposite of the miracle of compound interest for savings account.

Credit card debt = the menace of compound interest

Take a moment to list all your debt, the amount owed, the amount you pay monthly, and the interest rate you pay. Get this weight off your financial shoulders as quickly as you can, and you will be able to breathe again. If you have a long list of debt, identify those that you must pay in full each month, such as your mortgage and car payment. List all other debt in order of their interest rates going from the highest rate to the lowest. Reduce your monthly expenses and then allocate more to pay off your credit cards. As you increase your payments to these credit cards, pay off the ones with the highest interest first and then work down the list.

INCREASE INCOME

We've already talked about increasing savings and reducing expenses, but there's one final area we need to hit on—an area that women overlook far more often than men. Your paycheck. It's common knowledge among HR professionals that men are more likely than women to negotiate pay when they start a new job. In addition, men ask for raises and bonuses far more often than women. For years, I was underpaid relative to my responsibilities. In looking back, some of it was me, not solely the company or my boss. As a prior HR executive, my observation is that many women (not all) are afraid to ask for a raise and believe they may be judged negatively. I'll let you make the final call for your specific role and compensation. I suggest getting online, talking with your HR representative and your professional association, and doing some research regarding compensation. The worst that will happen is that you determine you're fairly compensated. If so, congratulations! If not, gather data and develop a plan of action for a discussion about your financial value to the organization.

8

DOWNWARD DOGGING
TO ACHIEVE GOALS

Some of you have read this section with pride and relief. You're doing a great job negotiating pay increases. You're saving. You and your family control expenses. You've taken vacations the past couple of years. And, there's some money left over that you can use for extra savings or to do something way out of the ordinary.

Others have read this section with stress, anxiety, and trepidation. You're overcome with doubt and don't know where to start. Remember, you can't eat the whole pie at one time. You must slice the pie and eat it one bite at a time. You didn't get into this predicament overnight and it won't change in a day either. Write it all down. Set some goals and start on them; one step at a time.

As we will discuss later, stress is toxic. And, it's amplified when it could have been avoided and prevented. Credit card debt fits in this category and it doesn't get any better the longer you avoid it. It will impact your physical and mental health.

After my divorce, I worked and paid off debt. For entertainment, I went to free shows and found low-dollar activities. I sold my house and moved into an apartment. I called my credit card companies and cancelled cards and/or renegotiated my interest rates. I moved balances from one card to another card charging a lower interest rate. (Be sure to know the restrictions). I reduced the amount I saved and increased my debt payments. I didn't go shopping except for food, and I kept sending money in to reduce the card balances. A prior boss had a work saying: It was time for "nose down and ass up" ... with the image of a dog on the hunt. Put your head down and work. Or, as I say, using a yoga term, "I was downward dogging all day long!" It's amazing how resourceful we can be when circumstances require it.

If you want to have better knowledge of your finances, start paying attention. Make use of tools from your bank, software such as Quicken, an Excel spreadsheet, or an app. Track information like how much money is coming in and how much is paid out in taxes or for insurance. After a while, you'll get a feel of the normal flow of your money. I've had clients who can speak from memory about their cash flow, others that use a notepad, and those who don't have a clue. Let me suggest it's important to have a clue, but you don't need to have the details memorized.

When I was a financial advisor, friends asked me all the time if they had enough money to retire. They'd tell me how much they had saved and how old they were. If they were close friends, I might even play along and ask more questions. *Do you plan on staying married? Will you have more kids? Have a mortgage? Other debt? How much do you make? What do you think the rate of inflation will be? How long will you live?* Unfortunately, my answer was always the same, "I have no idea." I love financial planning. I'm a planner, but there are so many variables that one cannot give a dollar number on the fly. Furthermore, it depends on lifestyle—what is it now and what do you want it to be in the future? My friend who owns a catering business tells me she can go from "beanies and weenies to caviar." The same is true for lifestyles. It's worth the money to work with a financial advisor and/or Certified Financial Planner (CFP) to help solve these many questions. We are living longer, experiencing more, traveling around the globe, and are at risk for significant health costs, which are rising three times the rate of general inflation.

When we talk about money and longevity, we mean this in two contexts:

- The length of life, and more specifically the length you'd like your life to be
- The lifestyle you'd like during your life

Why? When we think about financial requirements, living a long life of sacrifice and austerity may be simpler to accomplish than a long life that includes multiple homes and extensive international travel. Do you have the lifestyle you'd like now? Can you envision what life will be like at 60 or 70 years old - or as we say in our house, when you're a "Super Adult"?

Marketing lures us to spend. Our economy grows because of it, but you personally do not have to carry the weight of the U.S. economy on your shoulders. Learn to spend less than you earn, every day, every paycheck, over time — and start today. Ask yourself:

- What would be the easiest money habit you could start today?
- What would you gain from this new habit?
- Do you need anyone's help or cooperation?
- What exactly are you going to do?
- When are you going to start?

Congratulations! By working through this detailed section, you have either taken a big step forward in your financial literacy or have confirmed what you already knew. I'm cheering you on to make one positive long-term decision about your money. It will make an amazing difference in your life, now and in the future.

Write down two actions you can take this week related to improving your finances:

1)

2)

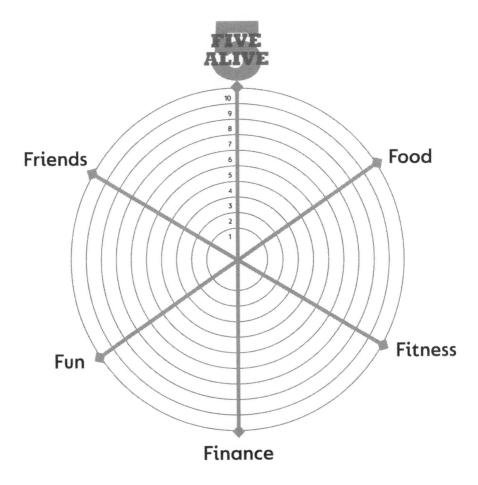

FINANCE SECTION SUMMARY

1) We learn money habits from the money messages we're taught or observe from others.

2) Define what "rich" and "wealthy" mean to you.

3) Calculate how much savings you have and how much you need.

4) Never stop saving; increase and decrease as needed, but never stop.

5) Know approximately how much your monthly expenses are.

6) Today's paycheck = Today's lifestyle and expenses + Retirement lifestyle and expenses.

7) Reduce and control debt—home, cars, credit cards—all of it.

SECTION II
FOOD

"Being a healthy woman isn't about getting on the scale or measuring your waistline. We need to start focusing on what matters—on how we feel and how we feel about ourselves."
—Michelle Obama, former first lady of the United States

9

YOU ARE THE LEADER
OF YOUR HEALTH

Sometime in my mid-twenties, I looked at the scale, and I weighed 203 pounds. At 6'2, that would be trim, but to put it into perspective, I'm 5'2". I didn't get back on a scale for a long time after that. I still remember the day I was in Daytona Beach, walking to the ocean to swim, when a group of guys in a convertible yelled out, "Hey, Goodyear!" In looking around, I was mortified to realize they were talking to me.

I knew one reason I was overweight, technically obese, was related to untreated depression as a teenager, which led to recreational drug use and overeating with no relationship to hunger and nutrition. After a while, weight builds a wall around you and psychologically protects you. You realize that enjoyable foods are one way to do nice things for yourself when you perceive that the world is not being nice to you. I also had terrible blood sugar highs and lows. I attended five schools in five years as a teenager and didn't quite get my groove on until my mid-20s.

Why am I sharing this personal information with you? Almost everyone has struggled with their relationship to food and how it affects our body and our health. However, we rarely have positive and intentional conversations about it. In addition, women get bombarded with public, damaging messages about food through marketing and advertising. Think about the messages we routinely receive:

- We women can't handle our emotions when we get dumped and need to eat a pint of ice cream.
- Salads are feminine and burgers are masculine, right?
- Women are anxious and can't control temptation; we're weak and don't have willpower.
- In order to be attractive and worthwhile, we must also be restrictive, healthy, and skinny.

The reality is that you must clear away these marketing and media messages and begin to tune in to yourself and your own body. Your body makes things challenging. It changes how it processes food and stores energy through your whole life. Often, women's issues with weight are rooted in not changing our habits to meet our new needs as our body changes. It seems no one told us the full rules of the game, did they?

This is *not* a book about adolescence, depression, eating disorders, or how to lose weight. It's about being healthy. It's about how to *become* healthy or healthier. It's about being in tune with your body's nutritional needs, about making better choices. It's about the continual learning process of improving one's health, sleeping better, having more energy, getting moving, getting rid of brain fog, reaching for better foods, and doing all that with a variety of friends. You deserve to know what feeling good feels like, and I hope you want to learn about food options that help you achieve this goal. When you begin to be more conscious of your health, you gradually adjust, and over time, you may affect not only how you feel today, but also your own longevity, starting with food.

Mudge Nudge: Start with small steps because small, smart actions compound over time and create big changes.

One would think that we as a society would place the health of our citizens quite high on our list of priorities. We might be a culture where we value health, and work to prevent disease. We know that it's less expensive to prevent poor health than to repair the consequences of repeated poor choices. We could teach people the benefits of healthful lifestyles. However, we are a system that responds to ailments, complaints, and problems that require attention and solutions. If you're lucky, you have exceptional health-care coverage and like and respect your doctors and health-care providers. If you're lucky, you're relatively healthy. Yet, even with that backdrop, you may not have received guidance about your nutrition and eating habits or the amount and type of exercise you need, and it's likely you have not been asked by a physician about caring relationships in your life - which are also important to your overall health.

It's with that premise that we begin.

We're the leaders of our own health project. You're the leader of your health. So, put out your Project Manager sign, and let's meet in the kitchen.

10

YOU'D LIKE TO MAKE SOME IMPROVEMENTS, YES?

We all need to eat every day. Let's agree we have that in common. What's your relationship with food? What does food mean to you? Is food associated with family and friends or is it simply sustenance? Is it associated with comfort? Is it related to entertainment and going out?

Most eating habits are developed early, particularly in our first five years. I'll assume that food was not scarce in your home and you had palatable food available for meals and snacks. In an ideal childhood, many different types of food were available when you were growing up. You were comfortable asking for more food and you were not chastised for not finishing everything on your plate. There was an understanding as a kid that your palate would change over time, so your parents were flexible with your eating without preparing special meals for you. You were neither a picky eater, nor were you required to eat all foods served to you. As you got older and started going out with friends, you continued to eat fairly balanced meals. You didn't need to binge eat the foods you couldn't get at home. This pattern became the norm through adulthood.

WAIT? What? That wasn't your reality at home or when you ate out? Maybe, maybe not! Let's assume that our folks and caregivers had food issues of their own. They brought this to the kitchen and the dining table, and influenced our eating patterns. A vegetarian friend got distraught when she found out her high school son usually ate bacon double cheeseburgers when he was out with the guys. Our relationship with food doesn't need to be labeled as "good" or "bad." It just is.

The catch is, what would we like it to be? Many of us beat ourselves up with negative self-talk that we could be better, that we have many improvements to make. When was the last time you heard a woman say, "I think I'm pretty good at that" (whatever "that" is)? We don't hear it very often even from our most-confident girlfriends. Let's begin with the premise that you'd like to make some changes and let's start with where you are now. You're going to create a Five Alive photo album.

11

A PHOTO ALBUM AND DRAGON FRUIT

Pay attention to what your plate looks like now. Start taking some pictures of your plate when you eat. Don't count calories. Don't measure servings. Simply photograph what you eat at home or when you go out. I recommend that you do this for one week and then look back at your photos in a Five Alive photo album. Also, take a picture of the inside of your refrigerator, freezer, and pantry.

Now look at and review the photos of your meals and take some general notes.

- What is the size of your plate?
- What are your portion sizes?
- Is there a lot of meat?
- How much fruit is there?
- What type of vegetables do you prefer?
- What color foods do you eat?
- What else do you see?
- Are you surprised by anything?

Are there any conclusions you can develop from stepping back and looking at your plate? Try to be neutral and non-judgmental. Give yourself permission to observe.

Select one or two of your meals to focus on. This time really drill down to specifics.

- Write down the individual foods on each plate.

- Estimate portions.

- Include condiments, sauces, salad dressings.

- Jot down whether you ate bread or rolls and/or butter.

- How about beer or a glass of wine? Add it to the list.

Now that you have this information, if you'd like to take a third, deeper step, get online and try to calculate the calories for each item on the list. If the meal is prepared, you might get the details from a restaurant website or the preparer or brand, such as Trader Joe's or Healthy Choice. Don't forget to count the extra cheese or guacamole on the side.

If this approach is uncomfortable for you, find a system for you to review and assess your eating style that is in your comfort zone. The goal is to not trigger guilt or judgment, but rather get a feel of your current nutrition and eating routine.

And the answer is …

If you chose the calorie route, how many calories did you consume for one meal on one day? Any surprises? How do these photos make you feel and why? Most of us are in for some surprises when we analyze our food intake.

In sharing this exercise with others during Five Alive workshops, we don't ask for a show of hands; it's too personal to share and we respect that. Yet based on observation, we can say a few folks gave themselves credit for good eating habits. The majority of folks had a visceral—*cough*—wake up call.

We know that many people do eat healthfully and may require minimal adjustments. Nothing good comes from shame or negativity attached to food, and most of us have already been down that road anyway. Our objective here is to work together to make some positive new decisions about our food and nutrition.

We know that if we want to maintain our weight, our calories consumed should be close to our calories burned (calories in = calories out). Losing weight requires fewer calories in and/or more exercise to make the formula work. Sometimes it's not about calories at all. Some folks maintain their weight even when they're not eating healthy foods. So, adjust your focus to include how much you consume (calories) and *what* you consume (type of food). That's where the magic is!

Observation: In the United States, it's easy to overconsume. Period. We prepare less food at home. We eat out more often. We're served large restaurant portions and are surrounded by exceptional marketing. Overconsuming is one of our big challenges to work through together, and we should first fully acknowledge it.

Managing weight or losing weight and keeping it off for the long term is *hard*. The process is most successful when everything you eat is in a food diary. Whether it's in a phone app or in a little notebook, noting what we eat keeps us accountable to ourselves. Therefore, it should be no surprise that the abundance of weight loss programs include this simple requirement.

Surprise Payoff: Even if you don't need to lose weight, you'll begin to eat more healthfully if you record what you consume. Solely by paying attention, you'll make small and subtle improvements, which will make you feel better.

OK, so now what? Where do we begin? Start today and know it will take significant yet fun experimentation. Fun: You will eat a greater variety of food than you ever did, and the list will keep expanding. Have you ever eaten something adventurous? Was it better than you thought? You'll either expand your taste palate or you'll get some great stories out of your experimentation. If you have kids or grandchildren at home, be sure to include them and let them choose some new food to try and share. By the way, for me, that exotic item was dragonfruit. The outer skin is a beautiful bright pink and it has white fruit and small black seeds on the inside. It's a tropical delight. Who knew?

Experimentation is one benefit of the journey. It may be challenging at first, but after a while, you'll become accustomed to trying new tastes. If you include your kids in the process, they'll begin to miss the new foods if you forget one week at the grocery store. If you can, bring them along!

TV and magazine ads forget to tell us it's not about a number on the scale. It's more about how you want to feel. What do want your health to be in 1 year, 5 years, 10 years? What do you want to look like in the future? Visualize it. It's not too late to start. Give yourself permission to take small steps to adjust what you reach for and your goals will evolve and change over time. Why? You'll be changing your palate in the process of experimentation. Also, science, research, and medicine will evolve and influence what we learn about, and how we select, our food.

Try it. Start experimenting with new food. Now. Today. Why not? You've got nothing to lose!

12

WATER (OR, EVERYTHING ELSE IS JUST FLAVORED WATER)

Water. Intuitively, we know that all flora and fauna, including human beings, cannot live without water. Water is the *only* hydration our body craves. Isn't that amazing? We can talk about coffee and soda on and on and the pros and cons of the thousands of beverages available for us to drink, but our body only craves water. Everything else is just flavored water.

In the United States, we have an abundant availability of free and clean water. As such, many of us undervalue its importance. We don't need a special water filter, we don't have to boil it, and it's accessible from more than one faucet in most homes. We even serve it for free in most U.S. restaurants. We can start showing some appreciation for water by drinking more of it.

In theory, water has no taste, but with so many specialty waters available to purchase, we know that's not true. Water in every city also tastes a bit different. Start by drinking one more glass of water per day than you do now. Tap water may be fine in your town. You may also use a filter on your fridge if it has a water dispenser, or use a special pitcher, such as those with Brita filters. Don't spend too much money yet. Start acquiring a taste for water one cup at a time. It takes patience. If you want to start with one adjustment, begin by drinking a glass of water every morning soon after you wake up. Sleeping is the longest period of time during your day when you don't drink or eat anything. It's not called "break-fast" for nothing.

Mudge Nudge: Add bottles of water wherever you spend the bulk of your time—your desk, your car, on the counter—preferably within an arm's reach.

If you need to start with flavored waters, drink them for a short time, keeping in mind that the long-term goal is to enjoy drinking plain water. I used to work with a man who started the day with one mug and two large glasses on his desk. The mug was for coffee, and the two glasses were full of water. He tried to drink four large glasses of water a day at work. He didn't always succeed, but by having it right in front of him, he had top-of-mind awareness. He took two trips to the break room in the morning—for coffee and water—and another in the afternoon for water. I watched him walk by my office every day for years.

How about an enhancement at home? When you eat at the table at home, add a glass of water to everyone's place setting. Before long, you'll all be drinking more water.

Do you want a hack that will automatically decrease your appetite and improve digestion? Drink your glass of water with your meal.

Water is the only hydration your body needs. Remember, everything else is just flavored water.

After a while, you may need to buy a water pitcher or water bottle to bring wherever you normally work or play during the day. You'll be surprised how often you drink water when you've acquired this new habit. Cheers!

13

REALLY, FEWER "CHEERS"?

Speaking of "Cheers," we should discuss alcohol. It's challenging to discuss alcohol without seeming judgmental, but that's not my intent. The Lancet, a peer-reviewed medical journal, reminds us that, "no level of alcohol consumption improves health." All I can say is, "Darn it!" However, research related to Blue Zones, those cities or regions with the highest longevity, indicate that consumption of alcohol is related to longevity. Could it be that the interaction with friends is the healthy aspect of sharing a drink at lunch or as the sun sets? Hmm ... There's plenty of data to support that high alcohol use is associated with disease, however, there is no data studying zero use of alcohol. Said another way, there are a grand total of zero studies proving that alcohol consumption leads to good health. (Spoiler alert: The answer is yes—relationships are one of the *most* important aspects to our longevity. Check out the chapter on Friends.)

Invest a few minutes to consider your alcohol triggers. Is it stress, a long workday, or socializing with friends? If you choose to reduce how much you drink, what situations are the easiest to adjust? Start with the easy steps. Ponder this, and then start slowly making a few adjustments.

Let's be practical without overanalyzing, and we will ask the scientific community to continue their research. When it comes to alcohol as a food, well, it's empty. Alcohol has little to no nutritional value. It tastes good. We enjoy it. It brings friends and family together, but it's an empty calorie. As you record what beverages you've consumed, you may find yourself being more mindful about how much you drink. Just to remind you: it's easier to make small adjustments over a period of time. There can be tremendous social pressure to drink, and if you choose to reduce alcohol, you'll find ways to do so more comfortably with "mocktails" and water.

Here's my "mocktail" example: When I was 21, I worked in the Service and Parts Division of Chrysler Corporation and visited Detroit. There was one woman, me, with approximately 300 men that were meeting the company executives at a cocktail party. I went directly to the bar and made a deal with the bartender: "Let this drink include vodka, but if **anyone** orders a screwdriver for me, don't include any vodka." I was not going to be the person to overdrink with the executives, and everyone there thought I could really hold my liquor.

Fortunately, I don't need to resort to that now, but a bartender repaid me many years later when I confided that I did not want to imbibe one night. He made me a club soda with a splash of cranberry juice and a lime in a cocktail glass, and I felt more comfortable with my group of friends. It may be easy for some of us to say no; congratulations if that's true for you. If not, select an approach that's comfortable for you.

Mudge Nudge: If you do consume alcohol, try to choose a beverage that you can sip instead of drink—one that lasts longer means fewer calories consumed. An example is red wine versus white wine. Most folks find it easier to sip a red wine.

Observation: Alcohol has no nutritional value, but it tastes and feels good. Use your own good judgment.

14

WHITE FOODS = ADDICTION AND OVEREATING

Look around your grocery store and your kitchen. How many white foods do you find? Is it more than you find in nature? Probably, because there really aren't many white foods in nature if you stop to think about it.

As a general rule, white foods have poor nutritional value. What you usually see when you look around are refined white foods like breads, rice, sugar, pasta, crackers, fats (think Crisco), and their cousins. The refining process takes away their nutrients and leaves a simple, easy-to-prepare product, which makes refined foods tempting. And, they're *everywhere*. My mind immediately is drawn to my favorites: baked goods. What food do you think of?

But, let's not confuse refined products with carbohydrates, which are not all created equal. Unprocessed carbohydrates, such as whole grains and vegetables (also called complex carbohydrates), are our bodies' preferred fuel, and our bodies create greater demand for this fuel the more active we are.

Observation: Refined carbohydrates such as white flour, white rice, white sugar, and white fat have high calories and low-to-no nutritional value.

Your body needs calories, vitamins, and minerals to allow you to comfortably and energetically accomplish your goals each day. If you fill your plate with low-nutrition foods, you'll continue to want more food. If you want more food that has low nutritional value, there's a high likelihood that you'll gain weight and be unhealthy over time. It creates a difficult cycle as your body keeps searching for nutrition. This is the primary reason why there is a correlation between poverty and obesity. High-calorie foods with low nutritional value are less expensive than fresher and less-processed foods, and these empty calories lead to overeating and make you sick. You may not be sick enough to go to the doctor. However, you may be tired, get colds more often, sleep poorly, be irritable, and not think clearly because you're not consuming nutrients and/or your blood sugar is low or volatile. There will be indicators and symptoms when you pay attention to your body. Your body may be sending you signals. The trick is to start tuning in to these signals.

Have you had days when you were lethargic and moody? Could it be related to what you've been eating and drinking lately? We often live uncomfortably with effects without thinking much about the causes. If you'd like to track this further, jot notes on your calendar or start a food diary with notes. You may begin to see patterns of what you eat and how you feel.

THE TALE OF A POTATO CHIP, OR, HOW NATURE HAS BEEN REFINED AND PROCESSED

You taste the salt first and hear the crunch, and you're already happy. The oil in the chip has a good "mouth feel" with the crunchiness and flavor of the potato. Your body digests the simple carbohydrates and the result is sugar and fat in your bloodstream. Boy, that was a good potato chip. You reach for another …

As you reach for the chip, you're making many people happy and wealthy. Think of all the scientists, chemists, marketers, packaging experts, and sociologists working hard to make you want another chip! This is the true impact of processed food—and we thought it was just a simple potato.

You order a baked potato and top it with salt, pepper, grilled chicken, pico de gallo, and a small side of guacamole. It fills you up for lunch. Baked potatoes and potato chips both start as potatoes and may have about the same caloric value, but they are *miles* apart when we calculate the nutritional value. The chips will leave you wanting more food much sooner because you ate calories, but didn't consume nutrients. Give yourself credit for choosing the baked potato because you've made a good choice. It takes a long time to adjust your eating habits. Take it one snack, one meal, at a time.

Mudge Nudge: Processed and refined foods such as potato chips are not only tasty, but they're easy to grab on the run, which can make it feel like these types of foods are your only option when you're busy. One way to combat this is create snack-size packages or containers ahead of time to make healthy items equally convenient. Also place the healthiest foods at eye level in your pantry and refrigerator where they're sure to catch your eye. (Do the same for your kids or grandchildren at their eye level.)

Choose your favorite:

1. Salty foods
2. Sweet foods

Many of us have a preference for one of these groups over the other. But let me ask you this, regardless of which category you prefer, do your favorite foods include fat? I bet they do. Think about those potato chips (I know you want some now!) and think about cookies. It's not a given, but it's common to have salt and sugar cravings that also include fat. Start looking in grocery carts and check out what convenience stores sell. Every now and then you might find a banana or an apple in a convenience store, but it's certainly not the norm.

So many diet tips exist out there, from Women's Health to Paleo, from Atkins to Keto; however, I have yet to see one fully address our food addictions. Fat, sugar, and salt are hard addictions to break, and some say **fat + sugar is the hardest.**

To truly tackle food addiction, first acknowledge what you're up against. The food industry is doing everything it can to make its food unrealistically flavorful and somewhat addictive. Overcoming that is tough, isn't it? One way to start is to assess what it is that you need to manage in your snacking. Identifying and owning your weaknesses is an important step to getting them under control.

FAT

We don't like *being* fat, but we do like *eating* it. It's the fat that makes those potato chips we mentioned delicious. And the doughnut we ate this morning tasted better because of both the sugar and the fat.

Although too much fat is unhealthy, not all fat is bad for you. Our body does *need* some good fat to store energy, balance hormones, protect organs, and store and process certain nutrients. So, let's agree that a small amount of good fat is more practical than no fat. There are also two kinds of fats. Saturated and unsaturated, sometimes known as "bad fats" and "good fats." The American Heart Association suggests reducing the bad fats to 5%–6% of your diet. Why? There are so many reasons to reduce bad fats, but here are five of them:

1. They increase the bad cholesterol—LDL
2. They decrease the good cholesterol—HDL
3. They create inflammation
4. They are linked to insulin resistance and type 2 diabetes
5. They increase the overall risk of heart disease

Good fat, you say? Sure! Grab that bottle of extra virgin olive oil when you sauté the vegetables for the brown rice and quinoa pilaf. Create a snack of wheat toast with avocado, chili pepper, and lime. Keep some roasted nuts in the car or at work for your snack. Toss chopped crunchy veggies with hummus.

Open your eyes, take a moment, and be more focused and mindful with what you order and what you prepare. Get online and into the grocery store and search for healthy fats. They're out there, sometimes hiding behind the unhealthy stuff, but search them out. Your body will thank you for it one day.

The bottom line is that:

1. Liquid fats, such as oils from nuts and vegetables, are the healthiest fats to consume; think olive oil and avocados.
2. Most of us in the United States eat too much fat.

What are examples of foods with saturated fats? Lamb, pork, fatty beef, poultry with skin, lard, cream, butter, cheese, dairy products, palm oil, and the most prolific, trans fats. As you can see, they are *generally* sourced from animals or made in a factory (or in a "plant").

Better fats, those that are unsaturated, are sourced primarily from fruits and vegetables and include avocados, nuts, olive oils, and vegetable oils.

Food Secret: For better health, use fats from plants, not fats *made in* plants.

SUGAR

Sugar is sneaky. It not only tastes great, but it also triggers the release of serotonin, a "feel-good" brain chemical. Yet it's one food our body does **not** actually need. At least, not the refined kind, which is just another processed white food. While the body does require sugar for energy, the most natural way to get it is to eat healthy foods, such as fruit, and allow the body to convert those foods to sugar in a natural process.

If sugar's your weak link, it can be a tough battle to fight. Sugar is practically irresistible since it gives us pleasure. The catch-22, though, is that the more sugar we consume, the less pleasure it gives us with each additional bite. And that makes us want to consume more. Blame the nucleus accumbens part of your brain, which is believed to release dopamine, from which you receive a pleasure signal. If we try to break our sugar addiction, we have to replace it with other rewards and positive reinforcement until we break the cycle—but be cautious. That doesn't mean you should replace one addiction with another.

Where is your sugar coming from? List your top three sweet cravings.

1.

2.

3.

For many of us, eating less sugar is hard, requires patience, and takes time. Some sugar is obvious—like what you add to your coffee—but most is hidden. It's in prepared foods, so you'll need to ask questions, look online, read labels, and check the percentage and grams of sugars in those products. I once had a trainer suggest I consume only 20 grams of sugar a day for a week (that's about 5 teaspoons). Now *that* was a long, tough week! (By the way, the guidelines are 25 grams of sugar per day for men.) Once you start paying attention, you'll see that even healthy foods, such as protein bars, have sugar. Foods that taunt you with flashy packaging are the ones you *must* read because they're designed to lure you to buy. You'll become an expert at reading labels and once you get in this habit, you'll keep it. If you want to hold yourself accountable for the sugar you consume, go back to your My Fitness Pal app, Weight Watchers app, or your notebook and record it all. The first five foods on the label are the major ingredients in a food.

Food Secret: There have been strong studies showing the positive impact of meditation as a way to reduce or eliminate sugar. Slowing down and practicing some quiet mindfulness and meditation may be a route for you to consider.

Let's go back to the scale at 203+ pounds; that's when I realized I had a sugar addiction. Around that time, I found a book at a friend's home, *Let's Eat Right To Keep Fit*, by Adelle Davis[5] (originally written in 1954 and revised in 1970). It's an oldie that's still on my bookshelf because it made an impression. It challenged me to think about what I put in my mouth and to eat more nutritionally dense foods. Now, it's still part of my collection of many books and articles and employee wellness programs, not to mention therapists, physicians, and nutritionist interviews and sessions that have guided me through the decades.

With Adelle by my side, I eliminated sugar cold turkey. It was a long two weeks of my life—from 35 years ago and I still remember it! (While her book had a good basic premise, unfortunately, Adelle Davis is not the best nutritional resource today. Today's research has refuted some of her teachings. You might instead reach for Dean Ornish, MD, whose books are based on current research.)

Mudge Nudge: Move sugar products away from your reach and sight. Recruit a partner or friend to support and encourage you. Add more fruits to your diet to satiate your craving for sweetness. If you need to, include some honey and organic dates. Be prepared to feel better after a couple of weeks.

We're not alone in our sugar challenges. Can you relate to this? Have you observed this in others? I had no idea how much sugar I normally consumed until I started paying attention. It was hidden in every delicious corner of every cabinet, in the refrigerator and freezer—it was everywhere! When you begin to review what you have in your home and make changes to reduce sugar, you'll initially be surprised how plentiful sugar, sugar by-products, and sugar substitutes are in your life. However, by reducing or eliminating them, you'll feel better, less bloated, more alert, and confident.

Mind Game: You could focus on reducing the amount of sugar you consume or you can try to focus on increasing the amount of non-sweet foods you eat, or even try a little of both. Which approach is most effective for you?

It might not seem like it, but it *is* possible to eat less sugar. Once you're in the habit of reading labels, you can find other ways to reduce the amount of refined sugar in your life. You'll need to personalize this depending on how much sugar you consume now. The more sugar you eat now, the longer and harder it will take to reduce your dependence.

Sugar Check: Check the ideas below that could work for you, so you can focus on the suggestions you're most likely to try and repeat.

- ❑ Prepare more of your own food; you have no control over ingredients in prepared foods.
- ❑ Think about what triggers your desire to eat sugar. Write down what and where you eat sugar and how you were feeling. Think "trigger—behavior and reward" and replace this pattern with healthy solutions.
- ❑ Start reaching for fruit when you have a sugar craving. Have it handy at home and work.
- ❑ At the beginning of the week, make a fruit salad and eat some every day.
- ❑ Switch from soda to diet soda to water, or unsweetened tea.
- ❑ If you cook, slowly reduce the amount of sugar in your recipes or start getting recipes from more nutritious sources like Eating Well, Cooking Light, or Weight Watchers.
- ❑ Deliberately choose when you will or will not drink alcohol and try to drink less when you do. Seek support from your friends—and the local bartender. There's no nutritional label on alcohol for a reason.
- ❑ Give yourself permission to eat some baked goods, or whatever your weak link is. By having a controlled portion now, you may prevent a binge later.
- ❑ Don't have sweet stuff in the house. Period. If you're going through candy bar withdrawal, you'll need to get in your car and drive to the store. Make sugar inconvenient.
- ❑ Try to eat fruits and veggies five times during the day. (My secret is a protein smoothie with two to three servings of fruits and veggies for breakfast. Everything after that is extra credit!)
- ❑ Become familiar with the many words that really mean sugar: corn syrup, agave nectar, fructose, beet sugar, malt extract, rice syrup, sucrose, jaggery, and evaporated cane juice are a few examples.

Hocus Focus: Your brain doesn't know the difference between real sugar, sugar by-products, and fake sugar, which means that changing to a sugar substitute won't reduce your sugar addiction, and may even increase it. This even includes sugar-free gum!

Finally, we now know that sugar is inflammatory, and it plays a big role in heart disease, obesity, and diabetes. The American Heart Association guidelines are for women to limit added sugars to 100 calories per day (150/day for men). That's about six teaspoons per day, ladies. But Americans are consuming one-third of a cup to a full cup a day! Soda and other soft drinks account for about 30% of the total amount of sugar consumed by us. In order of quantity, table sugar, baked goods, fruit drinks, dairy desserts (think ice cream), candy, breakfast cereals, and sweetened tea comprise the remaining 70%. Think about which of these items are your biggest temptations and try to limit your servings to one per day.

SALT

"Please pass the salt."

Our body needs salt, an essential mineral. In fact, salt cravings are prehistoric and all mammals need salt. Heck, we know that ranchers even put out salt licks for their animals.

There is little evidence that people have serious salt (sodium) addictions, and they may simply have cravings. Salt is instinctual because our bodies require it for water balance and to control muscle and nerve function. However, it's recommended that we consume less than 1,500 milligrams of salt per day yet some of us are recording 5-6 grams per day (5,000–6,000 milligrams); you know we have a salt problem. Eighty percent of our sodium intake is from foods we eat that have been prepared by someone else. It's tricky and impossible to really know. One teaspoon of salt = 2,000 mgs of sodium. Here are the 30 top offenders according to Healthline.[6]

Bagels and Other Breads	Baked beans	Biscuits
Boxed Meal Helpers	Boxed Potato Casseroles	Broth/Stock
Canned Meats, Poultry, and Seafood	Canned Vegetables	Cold Cuts and Salami
Cottage Cheese	Frozen Meals	Ham
Hot Dogs and Bratwurst	Instant Pudding	Jerky and Dried Meats
Macaroni and Cheese	Pickles	Pizza
Pork Rinds	Pretzels	Processed Cheese
Salad Dressings	Sandwiches	Sauces
Sausage, Bacon, and Salt Pork	Shrimp—Packaged, Plain, or Frozen	Soup
Tomato Sauce	Tortillas	Vegetable Juices

Food Secret: The salt you add at the table is the addition you notice the most, and people around you notice, too. You can test this by reducing or eliminating salt when you cook. You'll see how much salt you consume when you need to add it at the table.

Like you can with other foods, you can track the amount of sodium (salt) you consume for two days. Go ahead and add this to your app or look at labels or check online and record this in your food diary. Is it more that 1,500 mg per day? If so, start making subtle changes, such as tasting your food before you add salt.

Hack: For at least two days, cook all meals at home and try not to eat prepackaged foods. Do not add salt to any food while cooking. Do not bake sweets, which may require salt and baking powder for leavening. Taste your food without salt to get the flavor of each item. Then, add salt to your food and re-taste it. Take a moment to observe how much salt you add until your food is seasoned the way you like it. By making this one change—observing your salt intake, you may reduce how much you need over time. If this is too drastic for you, then begin by reducing the salt you add to food while cooking over time. Also, reduce salt use at the table and eventually you'll crave less salt. You can control this process over many months.

Salt intake is highly correlated with prepared, processed, and packaged foods which are found in stores and restaurants. Restaurant foods are generally high in sodium, and fast foods top the list. So, if you are spending a lot of money eating out, it's very difficult to control your salt intake. It's not too late to reach for foods that you prepare for yourself at home. By making that one change, you'll significantly reduce your salt intake (and save a lot of money). In fact, you'll go out to a restaurant and notice how much saltier foods taste. Eating more potassium will help keep your sodium balanced while you're cutting down, so you may want to add more fruits and veggies.

Mudge Nudge: Cook more meals at home with lean proteins, vegetables, and whole grains rather than eating packaged foods or eating out, and you'll automatically consume less salt.

15

TO MOO, BAA, CLUCK, OR SWIM?

It's a personal choice whether or not you eat meat, and people have many reasons why they select a vegan or vegetarian lifestyle. Some households go through phases of high- to low- to no-meat consumption. Regardless of your choice and philosophy, there is significant evidence to reduce the amount of red meat—beef, lamb, and pork—you consume. Frequent government and other research-based recommendations are to eat red meat *up to* one to two times per week. This is followed by chicken and turkey one to two times per week, fish at least twice per week, leaving any open days for non-meat meals. Furthermore, the serving size should be no larger than three to five ounces, equating in size to the palm of your hand or a deck of cards.

Most of us know a few vegetarians or maybe even vegans in our lives. Making some of these healthy choices isn't as hard as it used to be. Managing your intake is even easier. Share a meal with some vegans and vegetarians, and you'll pick up a few of their cooking and eating tricks.

It's not too late to make small and ongoing adjustments in the amount of meat you consume. There's a plethora of data supporting the benefits of a vegetarian or reduced-meat diet.

- Improves cholesterol
- Improves blood sugar levels and reduces diabetes risk
- Lowers likelihood of obesity
- Reduces intake of saturated fats
- Lowers blood pressure
- Reduces risk of heart disease

Could any of these health benefits impact you or your family? If you reduced the amount of meat you purchase, which health benefits would you most like to improve?

Hack: If you reduce the amount of meat you consume, you'll naturally reduce the amount of fat in your diet. However, the big culprits of fats are sauces, fried foods, and dressings, and you should take caution with these products as well.

MORE ABOUT THE MOO

Humans are the only species that drink milk from other animals. Every now and then you may hear a pet or animal story where one animal adopts the young of another species and nurses the baby. Those stories are the basis for good social media and human-interest stories in the news, but they're rare.

During most of our lifetimes, the consensus view on dairy intake has changed, and it will probably continue to change. Baby boomers would never have considered giving their children anything less than whole milk. Today's generation not only consumes less milk, but it's generally lower-fat milk. They may also have soy and almond milk in the fridge. Going full circle, the baby boomers are now drinking low-fat milk, too! Was that a soy latte you were craving?

From pediatricians to nutritionists, some experts promote drinking milk, eating yogurt and cheeses, and using butter. This decision is best made on an individual basis. Even with the development of some delicious no- and low-fat products, pay attention to the fat content in the dairy products you eat. Similar to salt and sugar, fat is often added to improve the flavor of packaged and prepared restaurant foods. What would a croissant taste like without butter? Bad, it would taste bad. A mere 1 ¼ tablespoons of butter has about 125 calories, and an ounce of cheddar cheese has about 115 calories. To put that in perspective, an entire three-ounce grilled chicken breast has 125 calories.

Remember to read the labels on the products, not just the yummy descriptions and pictures on the front. Check out the fat content. Yogurts, for example, throw curve balls all the time. We have so many choices. Is it high fat with low sugar? Is it zero fat, but full of sugar? Is the cream on the top? Is it real fruit inside or more like pie filling or jam? If you're trying to keep your *total* fat under 30% of your total calories consumed in a day, it's difficult to do that if you're eating a lot of dairy products.

16

ME GUSTA LA COMIDA ESPAÑOLA

Have you ever had an opportunity to spend an extended period of time somewhere where people live differently than you? When it comes to meals, there's a lot to learn from others, and there may be quite a lot of surprises, too.

The summer of 2018, my husband and I spent three weeks in Granada, Spain, studying Spanish. This was a goal on my Life List. I'm still not fluent (he is), and we had some surprises that helped us continue to improve our fitness and eating habits. When we returned home, we were five pounds lighter and felt great. Here's why:

- We walked everywhere every day, expending 10,000–20,000 steps per day on cobblestone streets and walkways and up and down hills.

- Fruits and vegetables were readily available and cheap, much less expensive than our costs at home. When you eat foods grown nearby, the transportation costs are low and the food is fresh. (Think farmer's markets and local foods.)

- When it's in season, it's available and you really enjoy it because when it's out, it's out. Case in point, we love figs. The first few days we were there, we bought figs at the fruit stands and open markets. And then they were gone, but the ripe melons had arrived! After a while you look forward to what's in season and even miss items when they're out of season.

- The Iberico ham is a specialty in the region. It's cured for over two years and sliced so thinly you can see light through it, but it's served in small quantities. A sandwich may have two slices of ham, one thin slice of cheese, one slice of tomato on fresh baked bread and be delicious. Fresh, ripe fruit for dessert? Sure!

- And yes, we did eat gelato and ice cream ... we had to while the stores were open. All of the ice cream stores close September 30—just too cold to eat it, or so goes the local tradition. The first time we had it, well, we felt a bit ripped off. "Was this the kid's size?" Everyone was eating small cones with a small scoop of ice cream. I bet it was less than half the normal serving of whatever we get in our hometown in the USA.

- Finally, a small tapas was served when we ordered a drink. It's practical to have a quick bite before or while drinking alcohol. It prevents big spikes up and then down in your blood sugar. I can still taste the simple flavors of Salmorejo (pureed tomatoes), bread, oil, and garlic served warm in the winter and cold in the summer. And all of this slowed us down to enjoy each other, listen to the music along with a smaller, lighter meal of the evening.

Eating is woven into our lifestyle, and powerful social and cultural forces are at work, but we can and should still make individual choices. These choices can be incredibly important. Investing in yourself, being your own health advocate will make it easier over time to make choices of more nutritionally dense foods—even if they may be different than what your friends and family are choosing for themselves.

17

I NEVER ATE EGGPLANT

Let's shift to what to eat and why.

If you read any health-related articles, you already know to spend most of your grocery dollars in the produce department. The question to ask yourself is if you're willing to make small, ongoing adjustments of what you put on your plate. Or is it better to take medication and add doctor appointments to your schedule? It is really that simple. Furthermore, you can't run away from a bad diet, which means that even if you exercise on a regular basis, it will not be enough to compensate for unhealthy eating.

Fruits, vegetables, grains, and lean proteins pack more nutrition per bite than *all* of the food examples we've discussed thus far. Furthermore, you can eat <u>large quantities</u> of fruits and vegetables and consume very few calories, relatively speaking. Why? Because these are the nutritionally dense foods that are packed with vitamins, minerals, fiber, and micronutrients.

Without new habits, these foods may not sound appealing. However, if I offered you whole grain waffles with sautéed maple apples and an egg, you might just sit down for breakfast. If you could order huevos rancheros with black beans and light cheese on a corn tortilla, you might enjoy it. If a Greek buffalo burger with feta cheese, Mediterranean spices, and tomato on a wheat bun was on the menu, you might order it. You can season almost any vegetable and grill it with chicken, lamb, fish, and an occasional steak … now it's not sounding too bad.

A nutritionist once said, "A pretty plate is a colorful plate." Half your plate should be full of fruits and vegetables. Split the other half with complex carbohydrates such as brown rice or whole wheat pasta. Wrap up with a lean protein on the last quarter of your plate. Ask yourself if you have a colorful plate. When you've got this mastered, use smaller plates, like those used for tapas in Spain. If you go out to eat and they serve a large meal on a large plate, immediately ask for a to-go container and put half of it away. My Italian friends in New York taught me that it's OK to eat pasta for breakfast, so I'm comfortable with leftovers anytime. But if breakfast pasta is not your style, finish the second half as a snack during the afternoon or for lunch the next day. Do you usually have a lull about 3–4 p.m.? It might be time for a snack!

Another tactic for eating more healthfully is to reduce dressings and sauces. They add hundreds of calories and end up covering up the food, whereas the goal is to learn to like the basic elements of what you eat and then *enhance* the food with a sauce. As Julia Child said, "Rich sauces, especially the butter sauces and white sauces with cream and butter, should be used sparingly, never more than one to a meal. A sauce should not be considered a disguise or a mask; its role is to point up, to prolong, or complement the taste of the food it accompanies, or to contrast with it, or to give variety to its mode of presentation."[7]

Try your salad with dressing on the side … your chicken with the sauce on the side. If you cook at home, invest more time in marinades, grilling techniques, and more complex use of herbs to flavor foods. The best tip I received about trying new herbs is to use them in scrambled eggs first to get a taste of their flavor and if you don't like it, all you've lost is one egg!

Food Secret: Sauces, gravy, dressings, and condiments can add hundreds of calories to meals. Order these on the side and then dip your fork into the sauce and then into the bite of food. You'll still get the taste of the sauce on the food and you'll save a bundle of calories.

WHAT FOODS TO TRY

When we have Five Alive workshops, we ask people to get together and make lists of fruits, vegetables, and whole grains that they haven't tried yet. It's fun to swap stories of who eats what and why. Unfortunately, we cannot do this in the pages of a book, so let me give you a personal challenge. Whether you're the regular family shopper or not, head to the grocery store and buy three new items: one fruit, one vegetable, and one grain you've never eaten. In the next week, eat this food raw or cooked. Use a recipe or eat it on its own and either mentally catalog the experience or write it in your food journal. If it was terrible, don't give up yet. Go to the internet and search on the "best recipes for _____." Try that ingredient one more time. Ideally, don't select a recipe that's covered in cheese or has a high sugar content. Try it a second time. If you still don't like it, maybe you'll try it again another time ... maybe not.

Tell All: What new food/foods did you buy this week? Did you like them? How about your friends and family? Did they like them, too?

Next week, do it again. Try new foods, particularly fruits, vegetables, and whole grains. There are expansive options available now. For example, think about how many new apples are out there. Don't let those marketing dollars go to waste; experiment with new foods. Don't buy the expensive or exotic because if you don't like it, you're stuck with it. (Or, maybe pass it along to someone else to enjoy.) Eventually, you'll be searching (and maybe buying) online for other new ideas that may not be readily available in your town. You want to be in the position that the worst-case scenario is that you've wasted a few dollars and a little bit of time to figure out that you don't like something.

For example, I never ate eggplant at home as a kid because my mother never prepared it. Why? She didn't like it. Yes, parents influence what their children eat. Many of my friends were Italian, which meant that for a long time I thought eggplant parmesan was the *only* way to eat eggplant. Now I know better and enjoy ratatouille, baba ganouj, and cooked eggplant salad to name a few dishes. There's an old myth told that Arabic women must learn 70 different eggplant preparations before marriage. My response to that is, "Please invite me for dinner." (smile)

What about you? Are there foods you've never tried? Do you have any "hereditary" food aversions? Is it time to challenge them and try a few new things?

Mudge Nudge: Get new ideas and break old habits by checking out cooking classes near you, search online for dishes and meals different from your own ethnicity, and download or buy a new cookbook. Visit an international or ethnic market in your area. Talk to the shoppers there for meal ideas.

Check out the appendix in the back of the book for more fruit, vegetable, and whole grain ideas. Use this as a checklist to try those items new to you.

We can't control the gift of our genes, but we can control what we eat and when we exercise. The more we learn about our own health, and the health of our family, the better decisions we will make. With healthy lifestyle choices, we may be able to prevent and/or control future illness and disease. It is **not** a foregone conclusion that you will get diabetes, heart disease, or cancer like your folks, grandparents, or aunts, and uncles. You can choose to be healthier than your family, even if your mother never cooked eggplant.

Speaking of genetics, let me share a story. My dad's best friend, Mac, was not the role model for eating fruits and vegetables, yet he was always strong and fit. He could use his chainsaw with the best of them and mow the yard with no issues, well into his 70s (80s?). But boy, he loved his bologna sandwiches. This Kentucky Wildcat loved biscuits and redeye gravy, country ham, and eggs. He loved summer sausage and meat, and I can visualize him enjoying all of these foods. Mac never had a cholesterol problem, and I was jealous. He got the good cholesterol genes.

On the other side of the coin was me. I could exercise four to six times a week, shift to a practically vegan diet, avoid alcohol, and I could never get my cholesterol below 200. I started paying attention to my test results in my 20s. Lucky for me, exercise saves me because it dramatically increases my HDL (H= high = good cholesterol) and therefore my ratio of bad to good cholesterol is fine. I got half good and half bad cholesterol genes. I know that I must exercise and reduce fat and meats because I can't fight my genetics.

How about you? You probably have some natural challenges and advantages. What are they? Were you "gifted" with any challenges via your genes?

18

TO BE OR NOT TO BE ... INFLAMED

Ouch.

You turned the corner too quickly and ran right into the corner of your desk. You rub your leg knowing you'll have a bruise later. Sure enough, it's a bit swollen and the bruise is coming on. It will be even more impressive tomorrow morning. That's inflammation.

We know it when we have an injury. We know it when we stop our fall with our hand and our wrist hurts later. Lucky for us, this is inflammation we can see and feel. In simple terms, inflammation is a defense mechanism if there is a toxin, unwelcome chemical, or physical damage to your body. It's always on the lookout and turns on and off when needed.

"I'm not surprised you got cancer. You had a chronic inflammatory condition for decades," the oncologist said to me in passing at a checkup about my endometriosis history. This was years after I had ovarian cancer surgery and chemotherapy and I was dumbfounded. Could I have prevented this? How come no one told me 10 years prior, 20 years ago? Was this passed on to me genetically? Could I have eaten differently, exercised more? I was sad, angry, curious, shocked, and wanted to pound the table and yell at someone, "HOW COME NOBODY TOLD ME?"

OK, folks, I'm telling you NOW. The real serious inflammation is *not* the inflammation you can see; it's the inflammation you cannot see. It's the root of many chronic diseases, and I suggest you begin to talk with your doctor about it. I know now that I can control some of it. However, there is more "spin" than real data on inflammation; stay tuned.

I read, I asked questions, I scratched my head. The following year, I remember asking my oncologist if there were any foods to stay away from. He said, "Not really, maybe aspartame." That was the whole discussion. (I did not research this because I didn't use aspartame, except occasionally in Diet Coke; I switched to Coke Zero.)

Do you have someone in your life who seemed healthy and still had a critical illness? Most of us do. Have you intuitively observed what a loved one eats and think it may be a cause of some of their ailments?

Inflammation can lead to problems with our autoimmune system. This system influences the liver (our largest internal organ weighing in at 3.5 pounds), brain (our second largest internal organ, about three pounds), muscles and skin (our largest external organ; eight pounds) just to start. Asthma, thought to be a problem with constriction of the bronchial airways, actually starts with inflammation. That's why patients are given anti-inflammatory inhaled steroids.

When it comes to coronary heart disease, you may have heard about CRP or C-reactive protein, which is one method of measuring inflammation in your body. If it's the arteries that are inflamed, there is greater risk of heart disease, heart attack, and stroke.

Andrew Weil, the physician, author, professor, and director of the Program of Integrative Medicine at the University of Arizona, is prolific in sharing his views regarding healthy aging and developed an anti-inflammatory diet. His books were my orientation to the concept.

Here's the disclaimer, a big "however," that the magazine "Scientific American" said best in January 2018.[8] *While researchers have conducted many studies regarding foods and inflammation, the science on a specific anti-inflammatory diet is still out. We do know that alcohol is inflammatory for everyone. We know that a Mediterranean diet has been long endorsed by physicians and studied in relation to reducing or improving heart disease.*

A more general conclusion may be appropriate for you. Once you begin logging your meals, you might identify foods that make you uncomfortable. They may give you heartburn or trigger gassiness, bloating, or achiness. Your joints may swell or your thinking might be a bit foggy, and then you'll know to stay away from these foods.

Mudge Nudge: Check out "My Anti-Inflammatory Diet" experience in the appendix where I share my six-month eating plan to reduce inflammation.

Only physicians can "see" inflammation through exams, testing, monitoring, and trends. Schedule an annual physical exam—annual means *every* year. I don't care if you are nine feet tall and bulletproof. For all others, it's not too late to talk with your doctor about inflammation and your overall health when you meet with them.

Hack: My friend never works on her birthday. She spends the day on her health—her annual physical exam and blood work, eye exam, and dentist. It also includes a workout, a massage, and a meal with someone she loves. And, she never forgets the date!

I know a bunch of physicians. We talk a lot about health. In early 2019, a palliative care hospitalist told me about the prevalence of "fatty liver." The liver is cool. It's an organ that can regenerate if a portion is removed. (You know like a lizard can regrow its tail.)

People are eating such enormous amounts of fat, usually hidden in processed foods, that their livers can't keep up to process it. So, it does the next best thing. It stores it for later when it will have time to process it. The only problem is that the liver never gets a break and has no extra time. This means that lots of patients are sick with non-alcoholic fatty liver disease and will need a liver transplant before they're 60 years old.

But wait, there's more!

Twelve cancer types are associated with obesity, according to the International Agency for Research on Cancer: colorectal, esophageal, gallbladder, gastric cardia, kidney, liver, bile duct, multiple myeloma, pancreatic, and thyroid. For women, add uterine, endometrial, breast, and ovarian cancers. The real challenges are that these diseases are being diagnosed in younger and younger patients. There *may* be correlations between diet and these diseases. Check out your food photos and ask if there's room for some small adjustments to your diet.

My father grew up very poor and if it wasn't for high school football and basketball, he might not have ever visited a doctor. Later, the military took over his health concerns. Fast forward many years …

When my father worked in a large corporate setting, he and the other executives were required to get an annual physical for insurance purposes. The #1 Boss also got a physical; both he and my dad passed. However, while this was happening, #1 Boss's wife was not feeling well, did not have an annual checkup, and by the time she got to the doctor, her cancer was widespread.

Invest time in your own health. No one else is doing this for you. Be your own best health advocate. Learn when you're feeling good. Begin thinking about why you feel good. Ask yourself why you may not feel 100% on some days. What does stress feel like to you? How are you sleeping? Are you agitated? Do you feel energetic? Define internally what feeling good means to you. Get to know the patterns of your body. And get a checkup once a year; make an appointment in advance on your birthday. Please put it in your calendar right now, so you don't forget. You won't regret it in the long run.

19

TO BE OR NOT TO BE ... HUNGRY

Timing is everything.

A few thoughts about when and where to eat. As conventional wisdom states, yes, breakfast is important. Eat a little something even if you're not entirely hungry. Focus on eating when you're hungry, but not famished. That may or may not include three meals and two snacks each day. If you're the type of person who forgets to eat and waits until they're "hangry," set an alarm on your phone for snacks, to remind you to *consider* it. Why? Sometimes if you wait too long to eat, you're ravenous and you overeat. If possible, be deliberate and try to eat sitting down at a table. Breathe and chew while you eat. Is it possible to shift more calories to your breakfast and lunch meals? That's one element of why Europeans tend to be thinner than Americans. By consuming foods during the day when you're active, you have a greater likelihood of burning the calories you consume. If dinner is your large meal, and if you eat late, you'll have to work harder tomorrow to burn what you consumed today.

Men and women who have taken weight off and kept it off, usually learn to eat when hungry but not ravenous, as an ancillary benefit, a bonus, which may or may not be taught by their diet sponsors. Weight loss meal plans that include all prepared foods have this down to a science. It works until you go off their plan. However, the idea of eating regular meals and snacks with low-glycemic foods can work. (See more about low-glycemic foods that create fewer highs and lows in one's blood sugar in the appendix.) The ideal combination may be to use a meal plan and then, over time, begin incorporating food that you prepare until one day, you eat all your own prepared foods, and your habits have changed for the better.

So back to eating enough to not be hungry, but not so much that you're overly full. It's a good idea to learn to be satisfied. In Japan, there's a tradition to eat until you're 80% full, or *hara hachi bu*. The Okinawans are the best example of this philosophy and their multigenerational caloric restriction may contribute to their recognition as having the highest proportion of centenarians. They are also considered a Blue Zone.

A practical habit to practice is to assign a number to your level of hunger. That way, you can start being aware of your body and gain better control over your habits.

1. Not hungry

2. Somewhat hungry

3. Ready to eat

4. Starving—"Hangry"

If you're in the habit of eating when you're not hungry, you may be overeating, which creates a risk of gaining weight. You may be eating because of anxiety, stress, depression, or other reasons that you need to explore.

Are there foods that you're likely to eat when you're not hungry? Are there foods you'll eat when you're already full? Check your refrigerator and pantry. I bet they're within easy reach. It's a good idea to identify these foods, so you can be more mindful when you reach for them or choose an alternative. (And move them to the back of the refrigerator or cabinet, or stop buying them!)

If you eat when you're at level two to three, you're in the sweet spot. These are the toughest to differentiate. When you're at level two, you might say, "I didn't know I was hungry until I looked at the menu or smelled the food." When you're at level three, you might be eating bread at a restaurant or getting a bit antsy and ready to finish cooking your meal.

When you're ready to eat anything and everything in sight, you're in level four. You may not be able to control how much you eat because the reality is you've let your blood sugar get too low and you may eat fast. You're at risk for overeating because you can eat a large quantity of food in a short period of time. Your brain can't keep up to monitor whether you're satiated or not. In addition, your body didn't have fuel available when it became hungry, and you can begin to lose muscle mass if you do this frequently.

Let's Eat!

HUNGER LEVELS ➡ 1 - 2 - 3 - 4

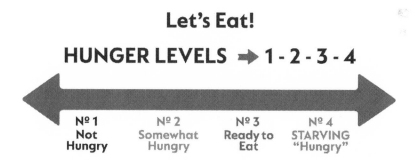

№ 1	№ 2	№ 3	№ 4
Not Hungry	Somewhat Hungry	Ready to Eat	STARVING "Hungry"

Key: Eat when you've reached level 2 or 3

It's not too late to start making small adjustments, changes, and improvements in what and when you eat every day. Relax and have a glass of sparkling water. Start shopping more in the produce department. Try a variety of fruits, whole grains, and vegetables. Set a goal for your plate to have more nourishing food on it by next month or next year. Change your personal culture of your longevity, one meal at a time.

Mudge Nudge: Don't head to the grocery store when you're hungry. Get in the habit of spending more time in the produce department and less time in the inner aisles of the grocery store.

Now, it's time for lunch, and I have a mix of chopped kale, quinoa, and hummus with tomatoes and vinaigrette. I like it. Five or 10 years ago, there is *no way* I would have purchased or prepared this. Lifestyle changes take hundreds of baby steps, small positive nudges, and time.

After about a month of trying new foods, take a look and observe what your plate looks like.

Get your camera out and notice the difference. Congratulate yourself for adding color, spices, and new flavors into your diet.

Mudge Nudge: On days when you feel really good, invest a moment to jot down what you had to eat in recent meals. Take a moment to appreciate how you feel. Mentally catalog it for future reference.

Two actions to take this week related to better eating:

1

2

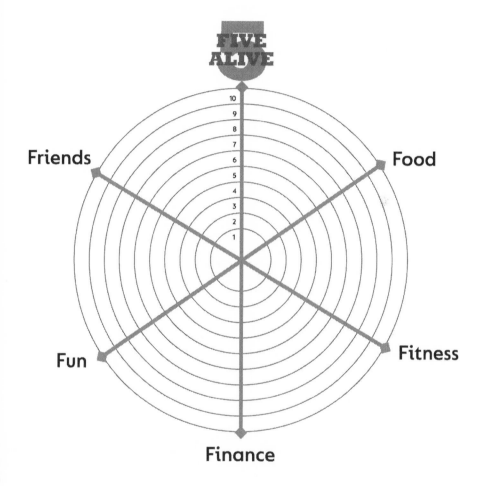

FOOD SECTION SUMMARY

1. Define what feeling good means to you and compare it to how you feel today.

2. Review what your plate looks like now versus what you'd like it to look like.

3. Water is the only hydration your body requires; everything else is just flavored water.

4. No medical studies proving the health value of alcohol exist; be mindful.

5. *Very few* white foods have high nutritional value; be aware.

6. If you have a sugar addiction, take it seriously and take measures to eat less sugar today.

7. Your pantry and refrigerator should include fruits, vegetables, whole grains, and lean proteins.

8. Eat when your hunger level rates two to three on a four-point scale; avoid eating when you're not hungry and overeating when you're ravenous.

9. Have an annual checkup on your general health, with a special focus on any diseases or conditions that run in your family.

SECTION III
FITNESS

"Take care of your body. It's the only place you have to live."
—Jim Rohn

20

THE BARBEQUE BELT

All of us have a sense of how fit we are. Whether it's 100% accurate or not, it drives a lot of our behaviors. Many of us have a "self-image" fitness level that helps us maintain our self-esteem. It may be an image you developed in high school or college that you still carry today. How do you rate your current level of fitness?

At a health conference I attended, the presenting cardiologist referred to maps on the screen. There were different gradients of color reflecting numerous health factors from high blood pressure, diabetes, obesity, and physical inactivity. He reviewed each slide and then overlaid the slides upon one another and with a broad stroke of his arm said, "And we call this the barbeque belt."

There were five states that were the brightest color: Alabama, Arkansas, Louisiana, Mississippi, and Oklahoma. There were four other states that showed up in three out of the five categories: Kentucky, South Carolina, Tennessee, and West Virginia.[9] As someone who likes barbeque, I realized he's right, that's where you can get good BBQ. When you let the data sink in, it can be quite overwhelming.

I scanned for the positive examples; which states were the role models? Colorado was the shining star in three out of four categories, followed by Utah in two of the four. Also mentioned in various categories were

Alaska, DC, Hawaii, Minnesota, Montana, and Washington. In the course of one year, I attended three health-related events and saw similar maps with each unique speaker, but now it had a name: The Barbeque Belt. I live on the western border of the Barbeque Belt. *I began my plan of action to move to Colorado. I have ski equipment, I have clothing for the snow, heck, I even own a Subaru, the "state car of Colorado." I have a ski and snowboard rack for my car. I would fit in perfectly! I would ski and snowshoe in the winter and bike and hike all summer. I would drink beer from microbreweries and bourbon from local distilleries. I would breathe fresh air, drink clean water, and enjoy blue skies every day.* POOF!! Then reality set in. My mortgage and my job were in another state where the cost of real estate and general cost of living is a bit more palatable. There's a trade-off for my choice of where I live … I live in the inactive Barbeque Belt. It's not only the barbeque that contributes to this recognition, but also our belts are longer thanks to our overall diet and lack of exercise. Do you live in an area that promotes health and fitness? Has it had a positive or negative impact on you? Could you be the leader to help your community become more active?

When kids see their parents exercise regularly, they learn that it's part of a normal lifestyle. Kids don't judge what's good or bad, it just *is*. When adults see other adults exercise, it takes much more energy to stimulate change. However, when a friend, a company, or community embraces activity, then there is some small nudging that is unconsciously cataloged. We may think, *"If so many adults are doing this, there must be something good about it."* If you have moved from an inactive Barbeque Belt town to a Colorado mountain town, the difference may be striking. It may even be a catalyst for questions and participation. Our health-care system will not take the lead for you; remember to be your own health and fitness advocate.

Mudge Nudge: Being your own health advocate is particularly important when you visit your doctor. We generally go to the doctor because we have a problem. Yet, it's wise to ask questions regarding preventive medicine. That is, what can you do to be healthier? Make sure your long-term health is getting the attention it deserves.

Let's take a moment to differentiate between health and fitness. Health is your physical condition and may be measured by a variety of tests administered by your doctor. A portion of your health may be predetermined by your genes. Fitness is a subset of health and refers to one's ability to perform physical activities. The elements of fitness generally include cardiorespiratory condition, muscle strength and endurance, body composition (BMI = Body Mass Index), and overall flexibility. It is possible to be healthy and not fit and vice versa, but it's more difficult to be fit and not healthy. Health is a snapshot in time, while fitness is a full-length movie that requires active and ongoing decision-making.

Think about how much you move now. Are you a runner or more of a walker? Do you walk around at work, do you lift heavy items for the job? Get out your Five Alive photo album. Start taking some pictures to show when and where you're in motion. Take a picture of the shoes you wear when you move. Don't count steps or check your heart rate, only document your body in motion. Do this for a week and then look back at your photos. What did you notice?

- Did you realize that you move a lot? How many minutes or hours at a time?
- Did the photos trigger some guilt?
- Did you spend a lot of time sitting? And did it include screen time?
- Were you moving more in the morning, afternoon, or night?
- Were you in a building or outside?
- Did you enjoy your activities?
- What kind of shoes were you wearing? Are they new, or worn out?

Mudge Nudge: Start thinking of exercise as movement and then add movement—take the stairs, park at the edge of the lot, carry your bags, walk faster, work in the yard.

The statistics reflect that only 15%–20% of the population of Colorado and Washington were inactive, which meant that **80%–85% of the people were active**. These two states were at the bottom of the *inactivity* list. The U.S. Department of Health and Human Services has established Physical Activity Guidelines at health.gov:[10]

- 150 minutes of vigorous aerobic activity each week
- Muscle strengthening two or more times per week

21

MOVE AND THEN MOVE SOME MORE

Aerobic activities are the first element of a well-balanced exercise program. Think of the active people in the active states mentioned above and relate this to your own starting point. One hundred and fifty minutes per week should be the goal.

Mudge Nudge: Now that you're motivated, pack your gym bag and put it in your car. It will be ready for you when you're out and about and you can easily stop at the fitness club. Squeeze in 15–60 minutes; remember, some movement is better than no movement. Achieve your fitness goals in small chunks that compound over time.

Fitness Secret: You do not need to be a member of a gym, have a personal trainer, or even perform rigorously scheduled workouts. You can be active almost anywhere. Some of the healthiest and fittest people you'll ever meet have never been to a gym. The secret is making daily decisions that favor activity. Walk to lunch. Take the stairs. Bike to work. These little decisions accumulate into a *lot* more exercise over time.

It's not too late. It's not too late. It's not too late. It's not too late. It's not too late. It's not too late. It's not too late. It's not too late. It's never too late to get up and start moving.

I like to travel locally and globally. Part of the reason I enjoy it is I like to people watch. When I depart from the Midwest and travel to the West Coast, I am pleased to see thinner more muscular people. I know some of this is attributable to weather and environments where temperature and sunshine invite people to get outdoors. Other elements are positive role models, demand for different types of foods in stores, community peer pressure, local and regional advertising, and events and entertainment that require movement and action. So, if you're like me, living in the Midwest, get out there and act like a Californian or Coloradan—at least your health will thank you! I have that same experience in most countries when I travel internationally. There is a shocking lack of obesity (although they're getting heavier as they add more United States-style processed food). People outside of the United States move more, eat significantly more fruits and vegetables, and eat less meat on a regular basis.

Mudge Nudge: Think of it this way: You can't eat a whole pizza at once. You must first slice it and eat one bite at a time. You can't run a marathon the first time out either. If your recliner or couch is your comfort zone now, make plans to get up and walk around the house, then walk around the neighborhood, then do it again.

150 minutes per week = 20 minutes a day x
7 days or 30 minutes per day x 5 days

(And if you're a high achiever, the goal is 40–60 minutes per day x 7 days)

You can do it. Think about the sports you liked as a kid or the activities you enjoyed. Want to skateboard? Go for it. Like the swings? Get to the local school playground or park and get started. Were you a world explorer? Get out on a trail or in your neighborhood and start exploring. Some cities have bikes to rent for low prices. Start by borrowing a friend's bike. Park at the edge of the parking lot and take the long route to the store. Think of ways to move. Lucky for me, I have a park as well as walking, skating, and biking trails right in my backyard and it has made a world of difference in getting me off the couch, away from the TV, and on my feet.

Secret: The easier it is, the more likely you'll get up and get going. Walk in the neighborhood. Meet a friend at the park. Keep your gym bag packed. Make it convenient to move more.

Last year I took a few months for a Fitness Binge. Do you have anyone in your life who's done something like this? Has anyone in your life inspired you with their effort? My goal was to be stronger, increase muscle mass, and decrease body fat. I biked, walked, skied, lifted weights, used resistance machines, hiked, drank only a tiny amount of alcohol, and carefully recorded my food intake. I met with my trainer once per week, and she truly challenged me. I lost a couple of pounds, although my goal was simply to get fit. And, I'm happy to say, I felt good and strong, and I accomplished my goal! When we met later to debrief and discuss next steps, I shared with the trainer that I wasn't interested in working *that* hard. I did feel good, yet I made too many other sacrifices in my life for this disciplined regimen. So, we agreed on a schedule and activities that were more comfortable for my schedule and commitment. What I learned, however, is that it's not *just* weight. It's about feeling good and taking care of myself while still living the life I want to live. It is about incorporating activity into my lifestyle. And, I became conscious of what *not* feeling good feels like. Lightbulb moment! And, because of this, I've learned that I like a lot of variety—both in foods and in working out.

Whether you want variety or one sport, check the internet. You can find hundreds of sports listed. Consider using the Meetup app to meet others with similar interests, or create your own new group for tennis, yoga, or other activities.

Mudge Nudge: Start adding workouts to your calendar. If you schedule it, you're more likely to get it done. And remember, a "workout" can be anything that gets you moving and challenges your muscles, heart, and flexibility.

Have you ever watched the Olympics? I watch them diligently, and it seems like I always learn about a new sport. Sometimes I wonder how it made the cut, but I still admire the athletes. Here are a few to consider:

curling, diving, equestrian events, fencing, handball, horse racing, judo, lawn bowls, netball, rugby, snooker, squash, and competing in a triathlon. Or, you could begin by walking more …

Mudge Nudge: Once you're moving more, try adding variety. Add some weight training and stretch more after exercising, or take a yoga class.

TV and video games won't kill you, but sitting will reduce your longevity. For instance, if we sit three to six hours per day at work, we shorten our lifespan, even if we have vigorous workouts. Consider buying a standing desk or a treadmill desk. Consciously get up and walk around, stand up for short meetings, and use the speakerphone or hands-free phone device when you're on the phone. I do wall push-ups when I'm on the speakerphone. Feel free to get a few stretches in while you're at it … no one will see you, but your arteries and heart will thank you later.

22

WELCOME TO YOUR 30S

Beginning in your 30's, you'll start to lose muscle unless you're incorporating resistance training into your exercise routine. The second element of a well-balanced exercise program may include powerlifting, exercise bands, or even using your own body weight to stimulate your muscles. By the time you're about 75 years old ("Super Adult"), you'll lose about 50% of your muscle mass, so you better get on it. Try weight reps with a can of peas, watch YouTube videos, or hire a trainer that demands a proper clean-and-jerk lift. Your legs need to be strong to carry your body. Your arms must lift and carry kids, groceries, boxes, and everything in between. Your core must be strong to hold it all together. Your abdominal and back muscles keep you upright, stabilize your posture, improve your overall balance, help prevent lower back pain, and protect all of your internal vital organs. Pilates, for example, focuses on total body strengthening, but with an emphasis on core muscles, and dozens of options are available to improve muscle tone.

There's another indirect benefit to moving and exercising more. Once you start feeling stronger, you get a bit self-conscious about what you're eating. Many people find that once they start paying attention to working out, they want to up the ante. They also start paying attention to what's on their plate. If you want to continue your Five Alive photos, and if you're feeling mission creep—that is exercising *and* eating better—take some pictures for the record!

Observation: Do you have gym gender stereotypes? Do guys lift weights and women do yoga? Throw it all out the window! We all need aerobic, weights/resistance work, and flexibility or stretching.

23

YOU NEED TO LOOSEN UP

Flexibility helps you move with a greater range of motion, which decreases your risk of injury and increases physical performance. After aerobic and resistance training, flexibility is the third element of positive fitness habits and is generally related to stretching. It's not the stretch you do first thing in the morning when you wake up with a yawn, although that too is helpful for getting the blood circulating and may stimulate the synovial fluids in your joints. A habit of stretching and flexibility exercises keeps your muscles supple. By reducing tension in your muscles, your body can move more freely.

You may use easy stretching to help before exercising. However, it's best to stretch warm muscles. Start by walking around, move your arms to get the blood circulating, and warm up a bit. I spend five minutes on the treadmill before stretching to warm up. This type of stretching should be comfortable and not strenuous; do not be in a hurry and do not stretch until it hurts. Cooling-down stretching is also helpful. First, slow your normal exercise *way* down. The goal is to get your heart rate slowed to a resting rate before stretching. You'll enjoy exercise more and by investing time in stretching, you can avoid some soreness and stiffness in the upcoming days and avoid injury in the long run.

Many types of yoga can have a positive impact on the body and joint flexibility. Classes at gyms or online, yoga apps, or videos can take you through some basic yoga moves. Eventually, you may develop your own yoga stretching practice. Many folks like the combination classes that start with heart-healthy aerobics, like a spin class, and end with yoga stretching. The same is true for Pilates that focuses on core strength and flexibility.

Are you your own best company? When it comes to getting in shape, you need to experiment. You have lots of options. Choose from classes, apps, and personal trainers at both minimalist gyms and sophisticated health centers. One is not better than the other, you need to find the one you'll go to! You have your own secret formula.

- Find something you enjoy doing. Or do you prefer to mix it up?

- Bring a friend to create a little peer pressure or to encourage you.

- Set small goals and when you reach these, make more.

- Some movement is better than none; while 60 minutes may be ideal, 15 minutes will always beat zero!

- Just get up and go.

Body fitness contributes to brain fitness, too. Although our health-care system separates physical health from brain or mental health, we don't need to follow this paradigm. Exercise contributes to improved executive function skills (frontal lobe), including taking care of ourselves, memory, and problem-solving as we add years to our lives.

Mudge Nudge: After you start working out, consider also making some adjustments to what's on your plate. Just saying …

24

YOUR BODY NEEDS
YOUR BRAIN

Can you keep your brain fit? Yes, you can have an impact. There are three elements to affecting brain activity: EBI.

1. **E**ngage your attention

2. **B**reak a routine

3. **I**nvolve multiple senses

What are you doing that challenges your brain today? Playing along with *Jeopardy*? Crossword puzzles? The app *Words with Friends?* Reading something outside of your normal genre?

Being curious, reading, investigating, and asking questions about topics you find fascinating engages your attention. Is it an activity you do once until the question is answered, or is it a longer-term interest or hobby? Go to the Board Game Café after dinner to try something new with friends to break your normal routine. Did you hike a trail with your geologist friend? I bet he showed you rock formations you'd never *seen* before, and he had you *touch* a stone with copper in it. Were you told to start doing crossword puzzles and sudoku for brain health? I bet you've been doing them every day for five years now. Now change it up.

The trick is if you're really good at sudoku, switch to crossword puzzles or something else. Think of your brain as a large road map. You can see interstates, neighborhood streets, and back roads running all through it. Your job is to take a new route every day. That's how you'll keep your neural networks fired up and alive!

Here are a few more examples to stimulate your brain:

- ❑ Ask yourself what brings you meaning and purpose. Do more of these things.
- ❑ Become a lifelong learner; learning and curiosity activate your brain.
- ❑ Discuss an article you read or something you saw online.
- ❑ Listen to a podcast or TED Talk or read a blog that interests you.
- ❑ Read—it stimulates the brain.
- ❑ Shift from same ol', same ol' to something new, something unique.

Elsewhere in this book you'll read about my experience with cancer, which I'm glad I'm here to talk about today.

After five rounds of chemo, I had chemo brain. I was pumped so full of chemicals that I would have bled antifreeze if I had a cut. But, I'm here to talk about it and to say that my brain's neural networks are different today than they were before my cancer experience. Chemo brain is not a medical term; it's not supported by research, and doctors are just beginning to look into what causes the fog or memory issues. I can only share my observations.

I've talked with others with very different health issues, such as a stroke or circulatory problems, who have shared some similar experiences. Suffice it to say, I've had many neural pathways restored, others rerouted, and a few that just don't function like they used to. I believe there may even be a few that are gone. Is it normal aging and perception? It could be. However, what's fascinating is that we can influence the health of our own brain. I would have never thought this to be true if I hadn't had a glimpse of this process myself. I take much better care of my brain now.

Mudge Nudge: Don't forget to wear helmets on cycles, skates, skis, and boards. Always.

Do you have anyone in your life who has had a visible loss of cognitive ability? It's easy to see how frustrating it can be for everyone involved … especially the person going through the decline. It's important we do all we can do to stave off this kind of decline. We have some "controllables" we can focus on to help us be more prepared for the uncontrollable.

It's not normal to ponder how we think unless there's some personal trauma involved. Whether it's chemotherapy, a traumatic brain injury, a new medication, or an illness that impacts our normal flow of thoughts, we may take *thinking* for granted. To challenge yourself, try to teach a skill of yours to a child or coworker. You'll realize that your thought process is completely different than the new learner's. Why? You've learned the skill over time through repetition, which created neural pathways for this specific skill. By the time you're halfway through the thought process and ready to teach others, your kids or coworkers may have already gotten the answers on Google. Everyone has their brain to thank for it - even if you take different pathways to get to the answer.

Fitness Secret: When you're learning new skills and really concentrating, have you noticed how tired you get? You might not even get out of your chair for hours. Right? Remember to move around before and during the process of learning new things. Your brain needs a lot of energy (oxygen) to function. Stay hydrated, be sure to eat (preferably low fat), and move around a bit to give your brain a break from all that heavy thinking.

Fitness Secret: If you can visualize the person you'd like to be when you're 40, 60, or 80+, you can become that person. Ever hear the phrase, "self-fulfilling prophecy?"

We are tuned in to the person we are today, and we forget that today's actions impact the person we're becoming. While I normally advocate for mindfulness and being present, it's imperative to realize that your mobility, flexibility, and strength today will impact your future lifestyle. Every single day, your food decisions and actions affect your body today and the person you aspire to be at 80. What would you like your mobility to be in the future? Do you have a role model more senior than yourself that you could look to for guidance? Look around at your friends, family, and coworkers. You see young people acting old and Super Adults moving around like they're the same age as their kids. Engage in your food, body, and brain activities so you can continually be curious and intellectually challenged. You may not notice it when you're in your 30s or 40s, but you won't be able to overlook the differences when you're over 50, 60, or 70.

Mudge Nudge: Choose the right mindset and role model now. It's not too late to start becoming the person you aspire to be.

25

BREATHE, JUST BREATHE

When we're stressed, our bodies release cortisol, which allows us to respond to stimuli with a fight, flight, or freeze response. This was useful at one point in our evolution; however, it's a bit different now that we're not face-to-face with a saber-toothed tiger. True, cortisol is an essential chemical needed for our survival. However, with too much of it, we may feel exasperated in traffic or snap at a friend or spouse. We may let our thoughts spin out of control and create stress for ourselves; it can have detrimental effects on our health.

How do you know if you're stressed? Can others tell when you're wound too tight? Invest some time to identify your indicators of stress: not sleeping well, irritability, dry mouth, heart palpitations, lack of interest in sex, overeating, undereating, digestive problems, and frequent colds or illnesses. One of my key stress indicators is that I begin to lose stuff, important stuff, like my car keys. What are your stress indicators? What are the people in your life noticing when you are under stress?

Other stress indicators:

- Are you feeling a sense of burnout?
- Are you drinking or smoking more than you used to?
- Is it tougher to make decisions or be productive?
- Are you feeling overwhelmed?

Once you realize that you're carrying a bag full of tension and stress, begin to remove the items out of the bag one by one. You may need help from friends, family, or coworkers. Try to be patient. You did not fill the bag overnight, and you will not lighten the load in a day. You must first begin to quiet your mind before you can create new habits. Here are some starting points to reduce cortisol and stress:

- Meditation—Research shows larger brain volumes and higher brain activity as a result of consistent meditation.

- Mindfulness—Quiet intention, living in this moment right now.

- Exercise—Take the edge off of stress and stimulate endorphins within.

- Digital detox—Put the phone, Kindle, computer, TV — all the screens — down.

- Get out—Switch from screen time to green time and go outdoors.

- Get out of your head—Shift your attention to others rather than focusing on your inward anxious feelings.

- Shut your eyes—Sleep seven to eight hours per night, every night, not just on weekends.

The Center for Healthy Minds at the University of Wisconsin, Madison, has completed research related to emotions and resilience. They found in their study and related studies that breathing meditation and loving-kindness meditation may not reduce stress per se. However, with these practices, people were more accepting of their distress, which helped them better tolerate situations that stressed them.

Many larger cities have meditation classes available to the public. Read books and watch YouTube videos. Or experiment with the *Headspace* app (or one like it) for excellent guided meditations and other resources. I started with reading about mindfulness to quiet my mind, and then took a meditation class. I sometimes use meditations suggested by the Dalai Lama in *The Book of Joy*.[11]

Fitness Secret: When you're in your fight-or-flight mode, you're experiencing high stress in the limbic part of your brain. Remember to breathe deeply a few times. This allows your brain to disconnect from the stress and shift to the frontal lobe of your brain where you have impulse control and problem-solving abilities. Take a moment or two to breathe.

26

AN ATTITUDE OF GRATITUDE

Once you've quieted your mind, make room for gratitude. With a sense of gratefulness, you'll have less mental capacity for stress. You'll have a greater ability for decision-making and problem-solving. With a slower pace, you'll recognize more enjoyment in your life and want to take better care of yourself. Physical and brain fitness are interconnected and you may have some surprising outcomes:

❑ Gratitude improves sleep

❑ Sleep reduces pain

❑ Less pain improves your mood

❑ A better mood reduces anxiety

❑ Relaxation helps you focus and plan

❑ Focus leads to better decision-making

❑ Decisions reduce anxiety and stress and increase enjoyment

❑ Enjoyment makes you grateful

❑ Enjoyment gets you up to exercise and be social

- ❑ Being social creates relationships
- ❑ Relationships reward your heart
- ❑ A warm heart leads to gratitude

It's not too late. It's not too late. It's never too late. Many of the recommendations and ideas shared in this section take a nudge here and there to trigger small improvements over a period of time. The process of making small improvements requires patience, forgiveness for when you fall off the wagon, and courage to reinforce your positive improvements. This is not a competition. **This is your life. It's taking responsibility. It's about the constant tweaking of your ever-healthier lifestyle.**

Mudge Nudge: A lot of dangers exist in the world and we can't avoid them. Let's control what we can. Don't smoke or vape, wear your seatbelt, and wear a helmet.

Two actions to take this week related to better body and brain:

1

2

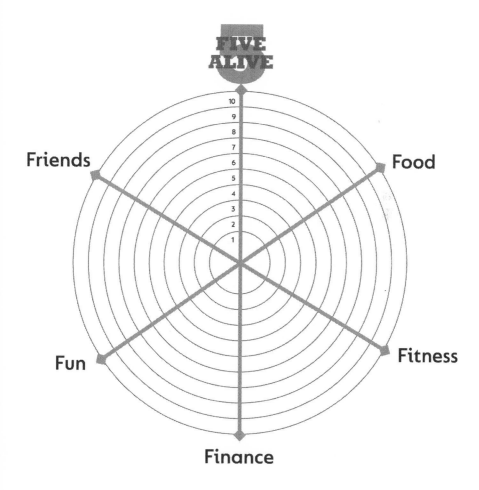

FITNESS SECTION SUMMARY

1. Fitness is a combination of heart-healthy aerobics + muscle strengthening + flexibility.

2. The goal is 150+ minutes of aerobic activity + strength training two or more times per week.

3. Make it easy to get your fitness minutes in.

4. Brain health and stimuli requires EBI: Engage your attention + Break a routine + Involve multiple senses.

5. "Your body ain't squat without a brain." Use your senses, try new experiences, and interact with people of differing viewpoints.

6. Know your stress indicators and start emptying your bag of stress. Did you lose your keys?

SECTION IV

FRIENDS

"All I can tell you today is what I've learned. What I've discovered as a person in this world. And that is this: you can't do it alone. As you navigate through the rest of your life, be open to collaboration. Other people and other people's ideas are often better than your own. Find a group of people who challenge and inspire you, spend a lot of time with them, and it will change your life."

—Amy Poehler

27

WE NEED EACH OTHER

Early hominids, the predecessors to Homo sapiens—human beings—were not designed to live alone. We're designed to help each other, learn by watching, collaborate to find and kill the wooly mammoth, and gather the food for our next meal. We could never do this on our own and survive long term. We are designed to identify synergies and accept and take advantage of the strengths and competencies of those around us. Early humans shared tasks related to food, clothing, and shelter for their group. Think about it, it's impossible to continue *any* species alone without reproduction of the species. Some animals live solitary lives except to copulate and continue the species. Humans, well, we need our clan, tribe, or community.

Modern conveniences such as the internet and smartphones have made it possible for us to live relatively safe and solitary lives. We don't necessarily need companionship and community for survival in terms of food, clothing, and shelter—we can order all of those on the internet. However, we still need the human bond and when we rely on technology, relationships with other people serve an even greater emotional purpose. We've come to realize that our long-term survival and longevity is really all about human interaction.

Scientific American said it best in an article titled, "Social Ties Boost Survival by 50 Percent." Here are a few examples that this meta-study, with over 300,000 participants, verified:

- Social relationships are thought to improve health by either protecting us from stress or creating a norm of healthy behaviors around us. A few examples are reducing disease factors such as lowering blood pressure, improving immune systems, and healing wounds.

- Friends provide a sense of meaning and purpose in our lives.

- "The greater the extent of relationships, the lower the risk," Julianne Holt-Lunstad, associate professor of psychology at Brigham Young University and co-author of the meta-study.[12]

It's true, there are people who are recharged and energized by connecting with others (generally called extroverts). Others prefer smaller doses of companionship and need alone time for recharging (introverts). Whether our tendencies are more extroverted or introverted, we still need others for our long-term survival and connectedness. We need a confidant or two—someone with whom we can share secrets and private thoughts. We need someone we can confide in and trust not to repeat the comments we share when we may be vulnerable.

Many more people are identifying as lonelier these days. Loneliness can occur in many contexts. We can be alone and not feel lonely, or we can be in a group of people and still feel lonely. If we retire or leave the workforce, it becomes harder to connect with others. It takes an effort to meet new people when there is no pool of coworkers readily available. In our later years, friends in our network die or are sick. You might not find it surprising that 25% of people over the age of 75 have feelings of loneliness. The big surprise is that the age group with higher levels of loneliness (~40%) are 16- to 24-year-olds—prime high school, college, and/or early work years. Is it just technology—that is, screen time? Yes, that's a part of the equation. Online friends are not as fulfilling as personal interactions because the exchange doesn't include elements of tone of voice, eye contact, or body language—all important aspects of communication. Workaholic parents model behavior that doesn't reward downtime. Even when a parent doesn't work for pay, many activities for themselves and their children are highly structured. We schedule gym time, happy hour with coworkers, book club, soccer schedules, and business activities outside of the normal time boundaries of our actual job. This leaves little room for relaxing alone or with friends or family. Does this mean we sacrifice talking about our values and concerns because our conversations stay superficial? It could, but you must be the judge of your own interactions.

Let's spend some time to better understand why people are lonely, and then we can address a few solutions.

- We try to substitute online relationships for personal relationships.
- Families are more spread out geographically than ever.
- Health realities can impact our aloneness—lack of sleep, sedentary lifestyle, and poor health.
- Mandatory overtime and being overworked creates stress and affects attitude.
- Materialism/consumerism, versus a relationship and people-oriented culture, places the focus on things instead of people.
- Delaying marriage means we may not have a close partner to collaborate with and confide in.

"If you want to go fast, go alone.
If you want to go far, go together."
—African Proverb

Some people are fulfilling their need for interaction by staying at, or returning, home to live. Others are sharing housing and communal living spaces. Restaurants have added community tables to make it easier to manage seating, and the side benefit is that it facilitates interaction with others. Research shows that making the effort to connect provides emotional and health benefits.

28

YOU'VE GOT A FRIEND

People with strong social relationships are less likely to die prematurely. Sharing our lives with others has a significant impact on our long-term physical and mental health. How? Interaction:

- Boosts well-being
- Builds independence
- Encourages new experiences and trying new things
- Improves mental health
- Promotes resilience
- Gets you out of your comfort zone
- Reduces stress and blood pressure
- Creates a sense of purpose

Invest in some time to self-reflect. Do you have enough relationships? Do you need more? Why, what's missing?

Friend Secret: We don't need to concern ourselves with the quantity of friends we have. Our priority should be the quality and depth of those relationships.

One person cannot fulfill all your needs, even if you've known them for many years, even if you're married to them, even if you knew them in the third grade. The people in our lives fulfill our unique needs—humor, companionship, caregiving, sports partners, problem-solving, health concerns, and maybe even fixing our plumbing. So, first accept that you may need more than one significant relationship in your life. You cannot rely solely on your spouse or life partner. It's not fair to them, and you know intuitively that others fill some gaps that your partner cannot.

Another important value of friends is how they connect you to certain parts of your life or a certain version of you. Childhood friends, college friends, and work friends, for example, all know a certain version of you. Staying connected to them is a way to stay connected to the "whole you." Are there people in your contacts list that you'd like to reach out to? Or are there people in your past you wish knew the person you are today? I raise my hand and say "yes" to both of these questions.

When I had cancer, I chose to communicate with only positive people. I learned to ask for support and was able to identify and enjoy many unknown skills I didn't even know my friends had. Some were better at doing, while others were better consoling and were comfortable sitting quietly with me. I had a close friend with lots of energy and I realized quickly that she needed to do because sitting quietly was not one of her key competencies! I needed people to drive me to appointments and cook for me and not be offended if I didn't like their food or fell asleep when they visited. These were valuable lessons that I retain today with a twist:

- Surround yourself with positive people.
- Do not judge your friends' weaknesses because if you do, in the long run, you'll have no friends.
- Identify your friends' strong skills and seek them out when you need that particular strength.
- Do not take people for granted; say "thank you."
- Remember to reciprocate—be a great friend.

Mudge Nudge: True friendships balance out over time; be sure to schedule friend time on your calendar.

If you've decided you need more friends, take time to improve this part of your life. Your family and neighbors may play a role. It may also be time to reunite with old friends. If you find yourself thinking you can't do this, ask yourself the following questions: *What am I afraid of? How come I'm not making the effort? What's stopping me?* Make a note of your answers and think through the best- and worst-case scenarios. Remember that reality is usually in between. Take a step forward.

Let's turn these answers into action by preparing a "friend review." List your top 10 friends in order, 1 to 10. Your list of 10 may move from a few close friends all the way to friendly acquaintances. Next to each name, add a grade between A and F on the quality of that relationship. Think about the A's and why you graded them as such; what are your criteria? Did you identify your confidants with high grades and acquaintances with a lower grade? Do you have a best friend that you could be treating better; that is, the score should be higher? Look at your C's and lower. Why did they get low grades? Do you feel responsibility for or blame others for this grade? What could you do to improve the quality of those relationships? Often, the answer to the last question is simple. It may be as easy as reaching out and connecting more often. Maybe you need to visit someone. Sometimes your relationships with friends require upkeep and maintenance.

	Name	Quality of Relationship A–F	How will I improve this relationship?
1			
2			
3			
4			
5			
6			
7			
8			
9			
10			

While this grading is subjective, I've also learned that my lower grades may be from hurt feelings or keeping score of who initiates contact. This forces me to think deeper about the friendship's value. It also helps me think about mutual expectations. I can then use these thoughts and feelings as I try to grow, fix, or rebuild a friendship.

Sometimes I think that creating new relationships is like sales prospecting: you must get dozens of prospects into the funnel to make one new customer. Developing new friends is somewhat analogous. We may meet dozens of new people, but that does not create a new friend. However, it is a good place to start. Let's think about pastimes, experiences, hobbies, interests—check out the chapter on Fun.

Building relationships means making connections with other people. To make it easier, we might as well start with people we have at least one similar interest or hobby in common with, right? This is where you take your fun realizations and turn them into action.

Associations, clubs, organizations, local blogs, online searches, magazines, Instagram, Facebook (or whatever social media sources), are all great places to explore. Start connecting online, in person, via Skype or FaceTime. Try new foods. Try something once, maybe even twice. Try a cooking class that meets monthly and get the vibe of the group. What's the culture and the mission? How does that translate to the people participating? Try to make a connection with one person. Contact a friend who worships where you'd like and attend as a guest to check it out. Attend a local Rotary Club meeting. Dust off your bike and head to where there's a group ride every Thursday. Invest time to translate your list of interests into real people, groups, communities, and places.

Mudge Nudge: As you start making new connections, try to identify what you like about each person and notice some of their interests. This will help as you try to encourage the new friendship.

29

COULD WE BE FRIENDS?

My friend Lyndon sets a good example. He's been interested in hiking trails. He read books, searched online, talked to folks at the sporting goods and local outdoor apparel, gear, and travel shops. Finally, he connected with a group in the community who liked to hike in the region. Over time, he made a few friends. Now there's a small group of guys he hikes with in and out of town. After spending time together, they learned they have many more experiences in common, and the cycle continues.

Where should you start?

1. Take the risk to start a conversation.
2. Create a communication exchange.
3. Identify common interests, traits, and experiences.
4. Ask open-ended questions; delve deeper.
5. Find similarities in others.
6. Decide to connect again.

As new friendships develop, they need to be cared for. Generally, you can't start a new friendship, forget it, and expect continuity and/or reciprocation. I put reminders on my calendar to reach out to people I like or folks I want to get to know better.

Hack: You can develop friendly relationships that connect to other areas of your life that you want to energize. Need more exercise? Find a walking friend or tennis partner. You can leverage this idea in any of the areas we're focused on in this book. Supper club! Book club! Investment club! You get the picture. Connecting fun relationships to areas of a current or aspiring interest is a great way to reinforce both the relationship and the interest.

If you were to make two style changes in meeting new people, first think about asking more questions. You'll have your chance to talk about yourself. Try to get others to talk about themselves first through encouragement and questioning.

First style change: Ask more questions.

- Tell me more ...
- Who convinced you to do that and why?
- What was that like for you?
- How did you feel about that?
- Would you give me an example?
- That must have been frustrating ... a relief ... fun ...

Second style change: Develop good listening skills.

Mudge Nudge: After asking a question, be sure to *wait* for the answer.

Before the championship game or a significant presentation, you invest time practicing. The same is true for good questioning and listening. Even the best questioners are often ready for a quick response, rather than sincere listening. Good listening may be the greatest contributor to building long-term relationships of trust.

1. Learn to want to listen.
2. Give verbal and visual cues that you are listening.
3. Anticipate exceptional communication.
4. Become a whole-body listener.
5. Take notes.

6. Listen now, report later.
7. Build rapport by pacing the speaker.
8. Control distractions.
9. Generously give the gift of listening.
10. Be present.

It's not too late; it's never too late to develop gratifying relationships around you. In fact, it's imperative. We'll have natural attrition in our personal community because people move and die, values change, and relationships expand, contract, and evolve. Your best friend 10 years ago may not be your closest confidant today. Life happens. We may also confuse acquaintances and true friends or work friends with people within our core group. The hope is to invest time to have unique and diverse people to weave into the safety net of your life.

Take a moment to identify people in your life who really listen. Who makes direct eye contact and leans into conversations? Who isn't just waiting for their turn to talk? *Be that person or commit to becoming that person.*

A friend of mine attended services in a local synagogue in Rome. He observed how touchy and chatty the locals were with one another. They obviously had not only known each other a long time but were also more effusive with their affection. He genuinely enjoyed watching these interactions. On the other hand, they did not extend their hand, nor open their interactions to my friend, the visitor to this sanctuary. Not only was this the antithesis of his own congregation, but also somewhat hurtful to someone who had come for a unique Italian experience. When we step away from this, we realize his experience would have been enhanced with personal interactions. It also creates a second lesson.

Secret: Even in this world of safety and protection, consider caring touches. That may include a handshake and grasp with both hands; it may be a touch on the shoulder or a pat on the forearm. Keep in mind that this may not be appropriate in a work environment, and you need to be sensitive with your judgment. In my observation, many people will welcome the small, personal interaction.

TIPS FOR INTROVERTS:

- Practice being the first to speak in a conversation with someone new.
- Remember that your questions will be what move the conversation along.
- Be genuinely interested. A conversation will always go well if you're paying attention.

TIPS FOR EXTROVERTS:

- Have planned questions ready to engage the other person.
- Make sure you really hear what the other person is saying, and not just waiting for your turn to talk.
- Be mindful of other people's sensitivities with regard to your talking volume and physical position in the conversation.

Sometimes we're the person looking for new experiences and new friends, but sometimes it's the person sitting next to us. Even if this may be a challenge for you, interact with someone you don't know. Be the person to say hello and reach out to shake a hand and introduce yourself. Be the person to ask what inspired them to attend the event. Be the one to try to find a common connection. The more you practice this, the easier it will become for you to start these interactions and engage with others when they reach out to you. Start being the person you want to become.

When I was facilitating corporate training, I attended a conference that taught me about stories. The message was that adults communicate via stories. I tell you my story and then you think, *That's interesting*, and you tell me your story. I had always included stories and personal testimonials in my facilitation, just like I do in this book, but I had never known why it was effective. However, I learned that I had to improve letting others tell their stories.

Stories are the simplest way to convey emotion and share personal experiences. Start observing people when they talk; you'll be surprised that it's fundamentally an interaction of swapping stories. It requires good listening, not interrupting or judging, and not trying to one-up the others with a bigger, better story. You may not be a storyteller, but I bet you're willing to tell me some of your stories. So … what's your story?

Out of the blue, I got an email from a CPA who served with me on the board of a local nonprofit organization. She reached out to have lunch. During our shared experience, she was professional, but a bit on the quiet side. I knew she was smart because she worked for a highly regarded accounting firm in town. We weren't particularly close, yet there were no negative vibes either. I was intrigued and accepted her invitation. I enjoyed our time together, and 90 minutes whizzed by as we got to know each other better.

I loved hearing her story, which included coming to the United States from Vietnam for college and overcoming many language and cultural hurdles. We came from such different backgrounds that you'd think we'd have nothing in common, but that wasn't true. OK, one stereotype is that we met at an Asian restaurant—which I love. She used chopsticks. I used a fork. We both like numbers. We both like business and client interactions. We both like being associated with nonprofit organizations. We both like to exercise. We both love vegetables. (I can still see the expression on her face when she asked, "How come Americans don't eat more vegetables?" We both laughed because that's a big message of mine in life and in the Food section.)

I'm appreciative for her sharing her story with me. Because of her mentor, and years of experience in the US, she now has the courage to call folks for lunch. She's even willing to share her story. What was most remarkable to me is that she commented that she was beginning to be the person she knew herself to be, just a version that's a bit more American. She had to spend so much time studying, trying to fit in, working to avoid making social mistakes, learning how to speak English, that she lost part of herself in the process. I'm grateful that she's finding herself again and that she reached out to share herself with me. She is truly working on being the person she aspires to be.

Are there people you may consider reaching out to, but feel that they're too different? We all have some conscious and unconscious biases; could these be holding you back? Traveling all over the world has helped me see and interact with many people who are unlike myself. Being married to someone from another country and continent, who speaks English as his third language, has woken me up to my privileges and biases. I've broken down some of my learned and unconscious barriers, but like all of us, I, too, am not without prejudice. I don't like this part of myself and sometimes it limits my perspective, therefore, I consciously work to expand my thinking. Take a moment to wonder why you may have similar feelings. If you can address them honestly, you can reach toward people who are unlike yourself and you'll be fascinated by and learn from their unique perspectives, cultures, and lifestyles.

30

THE CIRCLE OF TRUST

Who is in your Circle of Trust? Why? What traits do they have that facilitate a trusting relationship? Not all friends fit all of our needs. What qualities are important to you when you think about trusting relationships in your life?

Acceptance	Caring	Character	Communication
Competence	Honesty	Integrity	Keep confidences
Keep their word	Non-judgmental	Openness	Reliability
Responsibility	Sincerity	Transparency	Truth

- Who do you call with the good news about your promotion?
- When you need to vent at the end of a tough day, who do you reach out to?
- When the cancer treatment doesn't work and your dad enters hospice care, who do you share this with?
- Who's thrown a party for you?
- When you want to head out to a movie, who do you call?
- Who did you invite to check out your new apartment?

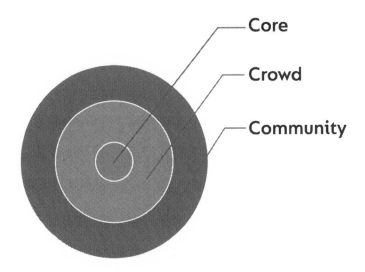

There is no magic number of people to have in your personal community, crowd, or core group. They don't all have to live in close proximity to you, yet some should be close by. They do need to be available when you have an emotional or physical need, however great or small. Take pictures of folks within your Circle of Trust and include them in your Five Alive photo album. These folks are your support network, your clan, tribe, kinfolk, and community.

Mudge Nudge: Make a list of characteristics you value in a friend. Why do you care for them? Why do you trust them? Why do you share with them? Look for those attributes and demonstrate them yourself.

Generally, your Core group is quite small and may include only a few people. My inner core know details about my life and death preferences that no other people know. They know my values, how I live my life, and how I aspire to live life to the fullest for as long as possible. We have an emotional attachment. My Core either know the other folks in the Core, or they know of them because of their importance in my life. They may understand the business part of my life related to estate planning or the medical part related to my advanced directive and living will. They may know the stories and memories associated with a few of my belongings that I hold near to my heart. I'm married to one of my Core players. Who do you share your Core space with?

My Crowd is larger, but not too large. I like to think of this group as those folks I'd invite to a special DECADE birthday party. Your Crowd may fit around your dining room table or may fill up your home. I've built memories with each of these individuals that may include a few inside jokes and nicknames. Some of these folks know each other or certainly know of the others because of our shared stories. When you visualize your Crowd, who do you see?

Community is the largest group in number and is a bit more diverse with respect to the depth of these relationships. It may include friends, some professional contacts, and acquaintances. It's people you like and enjoy being with even if you don't see them very often. They're positive resources for you, and they enhance your life in many small and large ways.

Spend some time thinking of specific people and where they're placed in your Core, Crowd, or Community. Who are they? Can you picture these friends and family in your mind's eye?

As you decide to add and expand your relationships, it's often easiest to build from the outside of the circle inward. As you move inward, there's a tendency to share more emotions. There may be a need for secrets and respect for privacy and promises made. This level of connection takes patience, confidence, heart, and a lot of trust.

Some people are so well-versed in relationships, they try to move us to their inner circle before we're ready. Others of us are hungry enough for love, validation, and support that we pull people into the inner circle out of impatience or desperation. Relationships are sensitive and dynamic. With some friends, you may pick up your connection where you left off. You may make a new friend and the interaction feels like you've known each other forever. The reality, however, is that bonds between people expand and contract; they flow and move and are not static.

31

SMALL TALK AND BIG TALK

One last thought, if you'd like to really get to know someone, do not wait to hear about them in their eulogy. I have heard myself saying, *"I wish I had gotten to know them better."* Kalina Silverman inspired me with her TED Talk about "Big Talk." Skip small talk and move to Big Talk. I have used her Big Talk question card game with dozens of people in numerous countries. I would bring the cards with me in whatever I was carrying. I would use them with my husband and friends, and even at parties. Generally, they were preceded by some small talk, or at least an introduction of the concept. Now, I don't even need the cards as a prompt, and there is no limit to new ideas for Big Talk questions. "How are you doing today?" turns into "What brought you joy today?" "What have you been up to lately?" is now, "What activities are you investing time in these days?" It may be as simple as expanding your follow-up questions … "What game did you go to last night?" "Who would you have given the MVP award to and why?" Try to develop a few new questions to use with friends—both new and lifelong.

The people in the Core of your Circle of Trust will be those you've shared Big Talk with for a long time. These are people you love and trust. You've invited them to your inner circle. May you all be comfortable there for many years to come.

Two actions to take this week related to enriching your circle of friends:

1

2

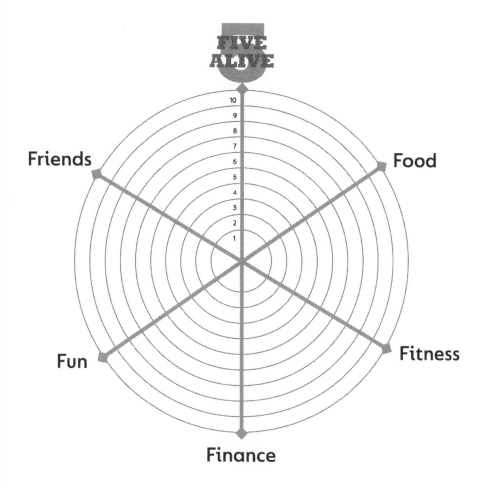

FRIENDS SECTION SUMMARY

1. People need people; our clan, tribe, kinfolk, and community.

2. It's not about the quantity of friends and family we're close to, it's the quality.

3. There is no one person who can fulfill all our relationship needs.

4. Start with small talk and progress to Big Talk.

5. Identify your Circle of Trust: Community, Crowd, and Core.

SECTION V

FUN

"We don't stop playing because we grow old;
we grow old because we stop playing."
—George Bernard Shaw

32

BRING BACK PLAY

What do you think about when you think of play? I hear my mother saying, "Go outside and play." I think of kids on a playground or kids and toys. I hear kids laughing. I don't visualize adults, or "grown-ups."

What do you visualize when you think about people having fun? It's an important question. Some people visualize themselves laughing with friends, some people visualize strangers having fun together, often we visualize children. What fun looks like *to you* is an essential question. Determining how to get more fun in your life is a worthwhile process.

We're going to dig in to doing just that in this section. Dear Reader, it's time to PLAY!

I was skiing with my husband and friends, and we all congregated where trails crossed. My husband was waiting for us and said we looked like a bunch of 10-year-old kids trying to catch up with each other and having a great time! Little did he know what a fantastic compliment that was to each of us. Our goal was to have fun, and he validated that for us. Do you have anything in your life like that? An activity where your normal "adulting" gives way to just plain fun? Think about it and think about how it makes you feel. I think we can agree that it's a feeling we all want more of. Let's make that our objective through this section.

Scientists have found that if they deny play time to the monkeys and rats they studied, the animals have deficiencies in their brain development. These deficiencies are seen in the prefrontal cortex, which is the part of the brain responsible for executive functions such as impulse control, emotion regulation, and judgment. Obviously, most of the animal studies on play and brain development cannot be replicated with children because of ethical concerns. However, social scientists have observed that kids who have more playtime develop greater social skills later in life. Activities for enjoyment and amusement with no purpose or goal would be considered play. Does that describe you? Do you have friends that like to play or have a sense of child-like fun? Isn't that kind of playfulness an attractive quality?

The Mayo Clinic promotes play as a way to:

- Reduce stress

- Improve your immune system

- Increase personal satisfaction

- Improve mood

We don't really need the Mayo Clinic to tell us that, do we? Most of us never feel more vital than when we are playing and having fun ... in whatever form that takes.

Secret: Often the biggest constraint to having fun is internal. It may be our lack of practice, our concern about embarrassment, or our expectation of how adults should behave. Sure, sometimes we have external constraints—maybe the board meeting is not the setting for play. However, think about being amused, generating fun, and finding a crack in the serious shells we all wear.

Give yourself permission to let your guard down, be a bit embarrassed on occasion, loosen up, forget your image or your ego, be free to have fun, and most importantly, throw away any preconceived notions about "acting your age"!

Hack: When you see a bunch of kids playing, you also hear them. They're talking, yelling, laughing, squealing, and smiling. Re-create that scene with a bunch of your friends and try to duplicate it the way kids do.

Take a moment to think of the word *recreation*. It is loaded with meaning: spiritual refreshment, amusement, new birth, "the act of restoring," "to make new, restore, revive," "to bring into being, beget, give birth to." Every moment gives us an opportunity to recreate. If you want the next moment to be different from the last, re-create it!

33

WHAT'S THE MOST FUN YOU'VE EVER HAD?

Eating, drinking, laughing, and having sex activate brain neurons that stimulate the pleasure zone in our brain. It is a survival trait. So, we could loosely conclude that pleasure is fun, or at least an element of fun. However, fun is highly subjective. It is based on our interests, temperament, and many other components of our personality. Some words come to mind thanks to dictionaries:

- Enjoyment
- Amusement
- Pleasure
- Entertainment

I don't know about you, but to me those words don't do justice to the word fun. What does fun mean to you?

-
-
-

Go back to your Five Alive photo album and add some pictures of people having fun. Include pictures of you out in the world having fun, too. In the pictures you find, check out the subjects' faces and body language. I bet you can tell who's having a good time. Let that be you!

You've made your fun list. Now ask a friend or partner to make their list of what fun means to them and compare. Fun is personal and depends on our experiences, our personality, and our temperament. What's fun to me may never make it to your list. What happens when you compare your list with others? I hope you find a few connections.

Mudge Nudge: Step out of your comfort zone and investigate events in your community. Attend one new event each week to learn, meet someone new, or experience something new and different.

From your fun definition list, create a second list of activities that you find fun. Are these in your photos or just in your mind's eye? What are the activities and situations that give you the most joy? Are there things that make you smile just thinking about them?

.

.

.

When compared to your friend's list, it's highly likely that you have a few of the same activities noted and that's why you're friends. What you consider fun doesn't have to be exciting or action-packed. It may not be all "fun and games" either but rather a topic, issue, or actions you're passionate about.

What fun *does* have to be is something that's interesting to you and something you enjoy. And you know what they say about time flying — when you're engaged in something fun, you'll often lose track of time.

Secret: The person you ride your bike with may not be the same person you travel with, but I'm sure you have fun with both friends.

Take the fun and activity exercise one level deeper. Consider the **past 10 to 20 years** and add experiences you've had in that time period. Think about the activities that were extremely fun. Remember your play history. If you need to, go back to your album and workbook illustrating your activities of 10 to 20 years ago.

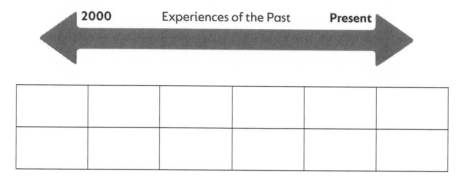

Were there one or two highlights during the 10-year period of time? If so, circle these items.

The last step of this task is to look 10 to 20 years into the future. Are there activities you'd like to continue or duplicate in the future? What about new events, experiences, interests, and hobbies that you'd like to pursue? Write these down.

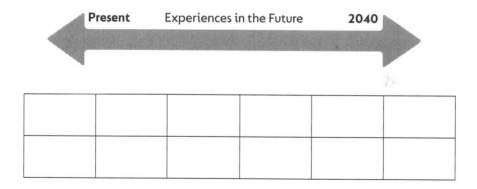

Why invest all this time on fun?

It's good for your body. It's good for your brain. It connects you with others, which, as you saw in the Friends chapter, is a critical goal to our positive longevity. We enjoy being with people who are fun … why not let that person be you? You don't have to be the life of the party, but instead aspire to be the person that people want to be around.

If you're over 40, adjust the fun exercise to cover today <u>to 20 years ago</u> and <u>today to 20 years into the future.</u> So, if you're 40 today, overall you'll be covering the time period between 20 and 60 years old. Go!

It's not uncommon for audiences to stop, tilt their heads, and wonder about the next 20 years. We may *assume* that we have more fun, interests, and experiences in our early years than in the later years. Why? Is that a stereotype? Is that what was modeled for us over the years? You don't have to behave the same as your parents and grandparents; you can design a future that looks different from theirs. Conversely, this is a good catalyst to think of people you admire because of their active brains, their variety of experiences, or their overall interest in living life to the fullest. Who are these people and what about them do you wish to replicate?

Let's make a decision to stack a lot of fun into our next 10, 20, 30, or more years. Maybe most of our fun is still ahead of us. Could that be true? Absolutely. It's a decision you can make and an action you can take.

Here's a list of fun experiences that others have shared at our Five Alive workshops:

- Snorkeling in Thailand
- Going to a professional sports game
- Teaching others
- Holding a baby or grandchild
- Dancing at my wedding
- Watching a son's first touchdown
- Completing a marathon
- Attending an outdoor music festival
- Hiking the Inca Trail to Machu Picchu
- Training my kid to ride a bike
- Traveling to Mardi Gras or Rio Carnival
- Seeing the Magna Carta or Rosetta Stone
- Eating at a Michelin-starred restaurant
- Looking up at the Milky Way on a dark night

- Watching all of the Academy Award-nominated movies
- Reading all of Toni Morrison's novels
- Hosting a BBQ for our neighbors
- Counting fireflies with my kids

It may be easier for you to start having more fun *after* work, but don't forget the hours you spend at work each day of the week. When you think about play at work, you may think of a bunch of people working in a tech company, shooting Nerf basketball or goofing off. My personal favorite at my job is the annual egg toss. Some of you may even wonder when the work gets done. You may have seen stories about how Google has incorporated play into its work environment.

Two words about vacation: TAKE IT! Over the years, I have observed friends get paid for their unused vacation days. In direct contrast, others (including me) have negotiated extra vacation days. You should know that I'm an incredibly loyal employee, and I'm not cynical. However, I learned a lesson from my father after I turned 40 and was considering a job change and feeling guilty about it. He said, "I've learned that I was always more loyal to the company than the company was to me."

After a divorce, after learning this lesson from my father, after cancer, after traveling to foreign countries, I decided to take this advice more seriously. Not only did I change jobs, but I also started taking more vacations!

To put this into perspective, let me share a bit more about the United States' employer vacation benefits.

- Companies have had mixed results when experimenting with offering unlimited vacation days. Employees tend to take less time because they don't know what the norm is, they don't understand expectations, and they don't understand if this is really about their well-being or publicity for the company.
- When surveyed, employees reported only taking half of their vacation days and working on 61% of their days off. (Glassdoor.com, 2014)

- When taking days off, millennial women experience more guilt than other generations of women and feel they don't want to burden their coworkers.

- The company FullContact provides a $7,500 vacation stipend to employees. If employees breach this by, for example, logging into their work email, they must return the stipend.

- There are numerous other examples of companies shutting email off to vacationing employees or after 8 p.m. on Fridays so employees don't work during the weekends.

As you invest time to identify people and activities you enjoy, you can begin incorporating them into long weekends off and vacations. Thanks to a friend's nudge, I recently went on a fun road trip visiting zoos and botanic gardens of three cities. She loves zoos, and I enjoy all things gardening. We ended up appreciating the other's interests during our six-day jaunt.

Mudge Nudge: Try numerous activities, as many as you can, in order to identify one or two that are stimulating and interesting. You might even be surprised by what turns out to be fun for you. Later, get out and try one more.

Dr. Stuart Brown, founder of the National Institute for Play, says that the opposite of play is not work; it's depression—seems reasonable to me. You, too?

There's a National Institute of Play, a book titled *Play*, a professional journal called *The American Journal of Play*, and even TED Talks about play. The irony is that some of the information is fun, but a lot of it is serious science. If you were wired up to a Functional MRI (fMRI), you would see that play stimulates your brain—and that's good. (An fMRI scan is a magnetic resonance imaging scan that measures and maps brain activity. It shows blood flow to display which parts of a patient's brain are being stimulated.) Play activates neural networks related to organization, problem-solving, creativity, and more. Stanford University has classes related to new product development, innovation, and play. Here's one of their recommendations related to making meetings more fun.

You show up at a meeting and are given a wearable, disposable white jumpsuit to put on. Each participant is handed a different colored marker. You remain standing and as you begin discussing the topic of the meeting, you make notes on your jumpsuit and on others' jumpsuits to record salient points. As you might imagine, most notes are on arms, lower legs, and the back of the suits. When you finish the meeting, you go back to your office. You take off the jumpsuit and hang it up because you'll need those notes for later (or else you wouldn't have had the meeting in the first place, right?). You had fun at the meeting, and you accomplished your meeting goal. You have fun when you recollect the meeting when you begin acting on your project, based on the notes on your jumpsuit. Is it worth less than $3 per jumpsuit, per person, per meeting? Maybe, maybe not, but that's not the point. I've had standing meetings where there were sheets of flip chart paper on the wall with everyone's name on it. By the end of the meeting, there were notes all around, and everyone took their respective sheet. You can do that on white boards and take pictures and send them to the team to work on their part of the project.

Secret: Remember that fun does not replace work. It enhances it.

To add some play in my office, I saved a funny card sent to me by a friend. I keep it at eye level. The graphics on the card make me smile, and it's a fun distraction when I get bogged down working on my computer.

What could you do to add some fun at work? Fun pictures or photos? Add a Nerf basketball hoop on your trash can?

Life needs to be infused with play that includes your body, objects, socializing, fantasy, and talk that transforms your thinking. The moral of the story is get up, play more, and stimulate your brain!

34

VISIT TOBOGGAN HILL

Take a moment to move around a bit and then take a breath to focus. Go back to your lists and shift to dreaming your dreams. What did you want to be when you grew up? What did you hope for? Who did you aspire to be?

Challenge your brain to remember or search for your unfulfilled wishes. Next, write down the experiences you would like to have in the next 10 or 20 years. It may be too late for medical school, but it may not be too late to get to the Grand Canyon—even in a wheelchair. It's your brain that stops you, so now is your time to wake it up!

(By the way, the Grand Canyon is wheelchair accessible. You may also access it via boat, horse, and maybe even skydiving, but the last one is just a guess!)

You now have lists of fun activities and experiences. If this was difficult, invest a few minutes to access and identify what you liked to do as a kid or at different times of your life (regardless of your age).

Many of us can remember moments when we were happiest. What were enjoyable activities and pastimes? Do you remember a time when you always wanted to try something special? There could be other prospective interests or pastimes to dive into.

Let's expand the list of potential hobbies and interests:

Acting in a Local Play	Bridge
Curling	Learning a Language
Pickleball	Sudoku
Underwater Welding	Writing a Blog

Note: As with any list I ask you to make in this book, the objective is not to make the list long; it's to make the list good. Make it truly meaningful, even if you only include two or three items.

When I was a kid in New York, I lived on a dead-end street. There was a basketball hoop at the end of the cul-de-sac. Behind the basketball area, you could cross a little brook and walk out to a field. It's now a bird sanctuary and it is *exactly* as it was when I was a kid. Lucky me; I loved this place. It was my personal refuge. Recently, I went back to see my childhood home and this area. I crossed over the brook, like I had a thousand times before in real life and in my memory. I walked through the field and down the hill to the Long Island Sound. I heard Canadian geese, just as I had 40 years prior. I was relaxed and delighted to be there. Because the outdoors is ingrained into my childhood freedom and experiences, I am still most at peace outside. I did not identify with this trait until I had completed the writing process of my past experiences, as you did earlier in this chapter. I then noted the experiences I aspired to have, and many of them were outdoors. This area is now the Jay Heritage Center in Rye, New York, but when I was growing up it was just "The Field" and the back corner was "Toboggan Hill." If you're in the area, please visit. But take my word for it: watch out for the poison ivy.

Can you associate the idea of happiness with a particular place? Go back in your mind and scan for locations in time that feel happy and joyful for you. Can you visualize a few places and scenarios that can still give you a happy feeling? That's how powerful "fun" can be. It can still reach you and affect you 20 years later.

35

GET BUSY LIVING
WITH A LIFE LIST

Finally, you may use some of these ideas to develop your personal Life List. Refer to this chapter and your lists and edit them over the next decades of your life. Since the phrase "Bucket List" originated by terminally ill folks that had to "get busy living or get busy dying," I lean to the phrase, "Life List." (However, I still recommend the movie *The Bucket List* with Jack Nicholson and Morgan Freeman). A Life List is for those of us who want to get busy living!

Feel free to use the list of hobbies and interests as additions to your Life List. You may also use potential activities for your future or pass these along to friends and family. Explore them, try something new. What's the worst that will happen—you'll waste some time or a few dollars? OK, now you know not to do it again. Conversely, what's the best thing that could happen? You just might like it!

Edit your Life List anytime. What are those special experiences you'd like to have? Are there places in the world or your state that you'd like to visit? Are there thoughts and emotions that you'd like to share with family or friends?

Start writing things down. Keep the list. Add to it when you have new additions, and scratch items off as you've accomplished them. Ask yourself why you haven't accomplished goals on the list and get busy putting together ways to incorporate them into your life. *I think I'd like to hike to the base of the Grand Canyon and stay at the Phantom Ranch with friends. I'd like a spa weekend somewhere—a whole weekend by myself. I'd like to go to a climbing gym. I'd like to spend one afternoon a week with kids.*

Mudge Nudge: Create your own Life List and start living it, little by little. It's not too late.

About a year ago, I was diagnosed with arthritis in my back. Yes, I had back problems for years, but the diagnosis upset me a lot. I asked the doctor to double check that it wasn't my hips instead of my back. He asked me why. I said, "I can get new hips, but I can't get a new back." That was part of it, but the real reason is that this didn't fit in with my image of how fun my life could be in the future. It took me some time to realize that fun includes my body, but it also includes my attitude and my brain. In conclusion, I didn't reduce or adjust my Life List. Instead, I adjusted a few of my exercises.

Most of us have had life challenges (health, relationships, work issues) that have made the idea of fun seem remote at times. Reintroducing fun as a priority is a way to regain control of the tone and quality you want in your life. "Recreation" is a powerful form of leverage. It reminds us that we're writing our own story, and we get to decide how much fun we want to have.

On the way to work one day, I was listening to National Public Radio. The person being interviewed was comparing the amount of fun kids and adults have. Adults may believe we need to grow up and be more serious, or we get embarrassed doing funny antics in public. There were dozens of reasons why these traits diminish over time. The program stated that kids laugh about 300 times per day while adults barely make it to 100 times per day. To combat this, John and Cindy Irwin invented "hilarity therapy" to help people learn to laugh more and find joy.[13] Laughter releases the "feel good" chemicals—endorphins. I was determined to share this new knowledge with my coworkers on the commodities trading floor. And for a while it worked, but we needed a bit of reminding to keep it going. Sometimes we even laughed for no reason, except to blow off steam, or to get a laugh out of someone else. Fifteen years later, I'm still trying to laugh more (let the count begin)! Try it sometime. You may be more comfortable when you're all alone and can let out a big, roaring laugh. I bet you'll make yourself smile.

The perception is that we have a greater number of fun interactions with people when we're in preschool through college. Over time, the fun factor measurement lowers or is forgotten. When we enter the workforce as adults, the fun factor changes—*occasionally* for the better, but usually the work factor beats the fun factor.

Think about how often you smile and laugh each day. More often than not, the number of laughs per day declines as we add birthdays. Life takes over and begins to include kids, mortgages, scheduling challenges, work travel, scouts, sports games, homework, getting food on the table, running errands, getting to work on time, arranging to get the AC repaired, getting some sleep, and then starting the process all over again each day, like the old movie *Groundhog Day.* Breathe.

Hack: It's hard to be mad, stay angry, or be down when you're laughing. Go ahead and try that laugh experiment again. No kidding; it works.

It takes about 25 years for the human brain to fully develop. The research regarding the development of a child's brain is expanding rapidly and triggers my curiosity. We know that play and fun are an integral part of brain development.[14] Playing helps us learn how to collaborate, experiment, explore, and solve problems. Why not use the same activities to exercise our developed brain? It's time to "Go outside and play!"

If you're reading this book, I suspect you're over 25 and have a fully developed brain. We have explored ways to keep moving for body health and shared ideas to engage and stimulate your brain. The ulterior motive for fun is to identify activities that interest you and activate your neural networks, and then use them as a catalyst to connect with others.

My personal motto is: "It is better to have 10 new experiences than the same experience 10 times." Now that I think about it, this may be more effective when posed as a question: *Is it better to have 10 new experiences or the same experience 10 times?*

There is no correct answer to the question, but there is a personal answer. Get out, have some experiences, and invite others to join you in the fun.

Two actions to take this week related to having more fun

1.

2.

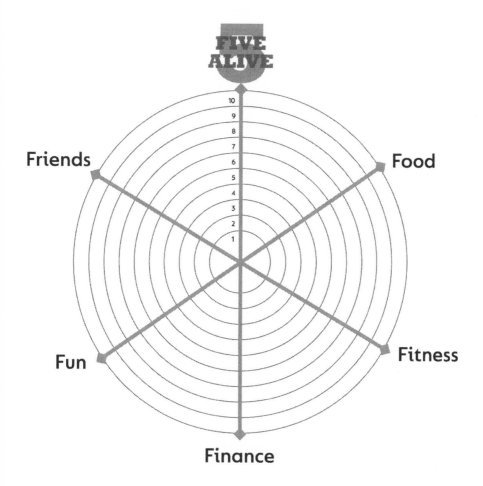

FUN SECTION SUMMARY

1. The opposite of play is not work; it's depression.

2. Fun is subjective and changes over time. What makes you smile? Define and describe what fun means to you.

3. Think about what fun new experiences and activities you engage in now and those you will enjoy in 10 to 20 years.

4. Use new experiences, fun, and activities to stimulate your body and brain and as a catalyst for connecting with others.

Conclusion

FIVE ALIVE—YOUR FUTURE

Is today the future you imagined for yourself? How different is it from what you pictured when you were in elementary school or high school?

I was lucky to attend college and even luckier to know exactly what I wanted—a degree in business. And then I wanted to work for a major corporation after college. From a career perspective, I was fairly clear in my goals until I reached about 40 years old. From that point on, I had different thoughts and phases of what my future would or wouldn't look like. At 40ish, I was old on a commodities trading floor. At 45, I was young in a financial services firm. I eventually used two sources to help me visualize my distant future. First, a 90-year-old man who was my role model. He was hunched over and used long walking sticks to help him walk and balance, but he seemed happy and remained extremely curious and highly engaged with others. I wanted that. The second source was the *Book of Joy* by the Dalai Lama and the Reverend Desmond Tutu. I tried the Dalai Lama's deathbed meditation. It sounds foreboding, and it is, yet the premise is to be able to look back at your life with peace. I yearned for that. I thought I could complete the exercise easily with my level of peace and confidence, but I couldn't. It scared the crap out of me. I had internal work to do!

Eventually, I was able to visualize the end of my life and even 30 years into the future (my expected life-end according to the financial plan I developed for myself). In full disclosure, I'm not always comfortable with this meditation, but I stretch myself in order to grow.

Have you had people, books, movies, or events that have helped you visualize your future self? Maybe you've used an app or social media to create the modified photos of your older self. Did you only focus on your exterior looks or your inner workings, too? It may have only been a glimpse, a foreshadowing of the person you aspire to be, yet all of these moments of realization connect. Over time, you begin to incorporate them into your being, your consciousness, your actions, and your behavior.

The exercise is the Dalai Lama's version of the "If today were your last day" question. Internalizing this question may create tremendous mixed emotions. My initial thoughts focused on the "wouldas" and "shouldas" of life. This was followed by places I wish I had visited and friendships I could have developed. I thought about a few items I would buy. Over time, my thoughts drifted from what was missing from my life to how abundant my life is. They went from loss to gratitude. It takes time, quiet, repetition, and patience for thoughts to progress. If you try this exercise it may help you unpack your emotional baggage from life or the baggage passed on to you from others. It helped me, but took time and practice. As of this moment, the only item on my Life List is to see Aurora Borealis or Aurora Australis. If the end is now, I would be disappointed, but more grateful for my wonderful life's adventure.

A lot of us have the "unqualified certitude of youth" and question our life choices as we age. Have you had that experience? Have you felt consistency in your self-confidence, or is it variable based on environment or circumstance?

Many of us think about our future selves as other humans or strangers … not ourselves. Today, it's much easier to go eat burgers and hot wings, forgo condoms, spend money, blow off a workout, or not spend time with friends because the "Future You" isn't really you. There's always more time ahead. Conversely, folks who have a strong concept of self-continuity see themselves on a continuum of self over time. They internalize the belief that today's behavior impacts tomorrow's outcome. This viewpoint is rare in the United States.

How do you improve your concept of self-continuity, that is, what your life is now versus what it will be in the future.

- Write a letter to your future self—20 years from now. What do you say?
- Establish goals for the future or develop a Life List (A Bucket List is for people who are dying, a Life List is for people living.)
- Do you regret that others are doing what you aspired to do? How might you change this?
- What's your most important wish and what's the best outcome? What's holding you back and what will help you accomplish the wish?

As you think about your self-continuity, you'll have some scary thoughts. The more time you invest in these thoughts, actually feeling these feelings, the better you may handle them in the future. When you get to this crossroad with a recurring negative thought, consider thinking about the:

1. Best-case scenario

2. Worst-case scenario

After you've done this, realize that reality is usually somewhere in between. While this is not always true, more often than not the results aren't nearly as bad or as good as you expected. By investing time in this thought process in advance, you become better prepared for all events. Over a period of time, you may even reduce the number of negative thoughts.

Here are some future-related examples that can be applied to this exercise:

- How are my eating and exercise habits affecting my future health?
- What's the likelihood that I'll get cancer? How far would I go with treatment?

- What if I'm alone after my kids grow up? How will I deal with that?
- What if I get some cognitive disease or Alzheimer's? How will that impact me and my family?
- Will I have enough money to put my kids through college or live the retirement life I'd like to live?
- Who will be my support network within my Circle of Trust?
- How long would I like to live? Do I need to change any behaviors to get there?
- Describe current and future pastimes and activities.

By reflecting on potential outcomes, you mentally prepare yourself to deal with future potential experiences. The hope is that by pre-processing, you'll better accept and develop an action plan. If this exercise makes you too nervous or anxious, then stop, as that's not the intent. Go ahead and put it aside and try again another time. The more grounded you are in the moment, the more helpful it will be to simply reflect. You can then put the negative thoughts aside until the negative event occurs—or, even better, you may not need them at all!

At the end of each of the five primary sections—Finance, Food, Fitness, Friends, and Fun—you were asked to note a couple of action items. Let's revisit those now. List the five areas in order of how you're feeling about your progress to date. We'll give ourselves a grade on each and begin to focus our attention where it will mean the most. Here are my grades from when I decided to become more deliberate about these crucial areas of my life:

Finance: A-

Food: B

Fitness: C+

Friends: B+

Fun: B

After grading how I felt about each area, it was clear that I had the most room for progress in Fun and Fitness. I narrowed my focus and started to make some decisions. I'm going to ask you to do the same thing right now. Ready?

Food: A – B – C – D – F

Fitness: A – B – C – D – F

Finance: A – B – C – D – F

Friends: A – B – C – D – F

Fun: A – B – C – D – F

After you've narrowed down to one or two areas to focus on, put this information in your calendar and begin to address your personal behavioral improvements over time. Adjust as needed, change your focus, erase, and redo. Create positive nudges to keep yourself moving forward. Be sure to give yourself credit for improvements to your focus on longevity and actions needed to improve and extend your life.

Visualize a new day in your future—a hike with friends followed by a meal out, for example. This simple pleasure includes the five behaviors I advocate: finance, food, fitness, friends, and fun. It doesn't have to be complicated, yet it may be atypical of what you're experiencing now. What does today look and feel like, and what would you like to experience in your future days? Begin now to adjust your perspective and by taking that step, you will influence the trajectory of your lifestyle and your longevity.

Appendix

MEN

With the majority of diet, exercise, and aging information directed toward women, a lot of men don't believe any of it applies to them, but that is incorrect. There's a reason that men's longevity is shorter than women's; men carry a higher health risk. With testosterone comes competition, machismo, less mental health support, higher rates of suicide, and cultural expectations for men to be big and strong to protect others. If any of these factors apply to you or the men in your life, we have an invitation for you to behave differently.

When I asked a fit 50-something friend about male health norms, his first answer was that men think being fit is lifting weights and being strong, even with a big belly. He believed that men don't have the pressure to look good to the degree that women do, and it's harder to motivate men to take their own health seriously. We laughed a bit about some friends who were high school and college athletes who still view themselves through this lens decades later. My buddy was that athlete, too. The only difference is that he's kept up his disciplined fitness routine since school. Thanks, coach.

Further, not all men want to bulk up, or come from an athletic background. Many folks, like my husband, come from a more cerebral upbringing, where brains were rewarded, and brawn was avoided.

Let's share some indicators of success for men.

- The Hillsboro, Oregon, police department practices mindfulness meditation to help them manage the stress of work, be more resilient, and have more clarity.

- From 1988–2018, men's longevity has increased from 71.4 years to 76.1. During that same period 34.8% of men are now obese versus 14.1%.

- Thanks to Viagra, there have been millions of additional orgasms in the world since 1998.

- Does the word burnout mean depression to some people? Employee Assistance Programs (EAPs) are now present at 97% of companies with more than 5,000 employees, and many of these programs include counseling and therapy.

- Want to have kids? Men can improve the quality of their sperm in 90 days by reducing alcohol, cannabis, and tobacco use; maintaining a healthy weight; and exercising regularly.

- Retired NFL running back Rashard Mendenhall learned to deal with his "Warrior Woes" (aka depression) with a combination of therapy, meditation, and philosophy.

Mudge Nudge: Disconnect. Your brain loves color and lures you to keep looking at the screen. Change your computer and phones to grayscale, and you'll be less attracted to them. Invest time in relating to people, not machines. (Yes, this is true for women also.)

Men, we need you to live longer. We like you, your kids love you, your partners love you, your coworkers need you, and friends and family desire to have many more experiences with you. Here are some ways you can do your part:

- Save more money for your future and current lifestyle.

- You don't have to be on a fad diet, but do reach for foods that are healthier.

- Reduce melanoma deaths by using sunscreen every single day.

- Add cardio work, stretching, and flexibility exercises so you can pick your kids up and play with them.

- Tell people how you feel about them, or share with friends that you may be having a tough time. This will not mean you have to turn in your masculinity card.

- Be healthy enough to qualify for life and long-term care insurance.

- Enjoy vegetables, fruits, and whole grains (if you'd like to reach 77, 80, 90+ years old).

If you follow this advice, with time, you may not have to wear your pants under your belly and you may also be able to recruit others to come along for the ride. And while these changes can't guarantee more sex, they will reduce the likelihood of fertility problems and erectile disfunction. (And the whole pants-not-under-your-belly thing certainly won't *hurt* your chances for sex.)

These dynamic elements lead to more questions to consider. Of the Five Alive behaviors, in which areas are you strong, and in which are you weak?

Which area do you want to focus on first? What would you like to accomplish? Do you want to improve slowly, or are you ready to change cold turkey? Starting when?

EMPLOYERS

There has always been an ebb and flow regarding what benefits to provide employees. Whether it's matching funds in a 401(k), on-site childcare, or health and wellness benefits to Employee Resource Groups (ERGs), employers realize they influence the overall well-being of their employees. There's a delicate balance between employee expectations and employer obligations and this fluctuates with social, regulatory, legal, and health trends.

New information shows improvements in employee health when they're involved with lifestyle management programs or Lifestyle Health Coaching (LHC).[15] The success is amplified if financial rewards are offered to employees for long-term change. The majority of participating employees include improvements in well-being, better health, and improved medical trends. It's tough to argue against employer-sponsored health plans, particularly when analyzing a potential reduction in health-care costs. When looking at obesity alone, once improved, there's a reduction in absenteeism, increased productivity, and lower health-care costs. And that's just one health factor!

As a prior business owner and corporate executive, I'm motivated by this idea from a sheer employee retention perspective. Hiring and training new employees is complicated and extraordinarily expensive. Why not retain team members with proven competencies? We know that diversity, inclusion, and equity programs improve profitability and performance in the long term. So, also ensure that your HR plans include varying generations, for instance.

There's a boardroom debate whether the employer or the employee is responsible for the health and longevity of the staff. I understand the comparison of real expenses to a potential future reduction of health-care costs, and that's a decision that I'll leave to individual companies. However, if I were still an employer, I would take a long hard look at the numbers from a sheer recruitment and retention strategy.

All aspects of the Five Alive behaviors linked to longevity can be adopted by employers as an element of in-house health and wellness programs.

- **Finance:** Support from HR and the benefits group, including the providers of the 401(k) plan to assist employees with budgets, savings, and retirement planning.

- **Food:** Food and nutrition counseling; food offered in company restaurants, snack bars, vending machines, and break rooms.

- **Fitness:** On-site health clubs, work/life balance programs, reduced membership fees for local gyms and/or fitness tracking that syncs with company and/or insurance records. Mental health should be a priority equal to physical health and should include more than three days of counseling through the Employee Assistance Program (EAP).

- **Friends:** Some work friends are superficial, yet others are long-term. Encouraging cooperation, collaboration, and interaction are all ways to build relationships between and among coworkers.

- **Fun:** Employee Resource Groups, affinity groups, in-house clubs, and associations all help people tap into their interests and hobbies. Supporting the local arts and social services communities encourages employee involvement and community pride.

Health, wellness, work/life balance programs are always exponentially more successful when they're enthusiastically supported by the leaders of the firm. When executives are visible role models of health and fitness, they send a message that taking care of oneself is as important as work itself. When companies include well-being goals in their strategic plans, they see an improvement in health and medical trends. Therefore, be sure to obtain positive commitments from leadership before implementing these new services and employee benefits.

VEGETABLES, FRUITS, AND WHOLE GRAINS

Below is a list of vegetables and fruits from around the world. Be inspired (versus intimidated) by all of the options. Some items may be available in the local grocery store, but you may have to visit ethnic stores and farmers' markets for others. The produce specialists at the store are your friends and will give recommendations of what to try and even how to prepare specific fruits or veggies. Farmers representing what they grow, well, you have an expert right in front of you! I have yet to meet farmers who don't eat the food they grow.

When traveling, be willing to experiment with new foods, particularly cooked foods if you're uncertain about hygiene and the quality of local water. You may also bring something to wash fresh fruits and vegetables, and generally, you can trust all foods in high-end hotels and restaurants. Were that not the case, I would have never tried azuki beans and dragon fruit!

Try it once, prepare it a second way, and then add it to the rotation or cross it off the list. You don't have to like everything, but, remember the eggplant story; you might just like it!

VEGETABLES

Acorn Squash	Alfalfa Sprouts	Amrud	Artichoke
Arugula	Asparagus	Aubergine (Eggplant)	Azuki Beans (Or Adzuki)
Banana Squash	Bean Sprouts	Beet Greens (Chard)	Beets
Bell Pepper	Bitter Melon	Black Beans	Black-Eyed Peas
Bok Choy	Borlotti Bean	Broad Beans	Broccoflower (a hybrid)
Broccoli (Calabrese)	Brussels Sprouts	Butternut Squash	Cabbage
Carrot	Cauliflower	Cayenne Pepper	Celeriac
Celery	Chard (Beet Greens)	Chickpeas (Garbanzos)	Chili Pepper
Chives	Collard Greens	Courgette (UK)/ Zucchini (US)	Cucumber
Daikon	Delicata	Endive	Fennel
Fiddleheads	Frisee	Garlic	Gem Squash
Ginger	Green Beans	Greens	Habanero
Horseradish	Hubbard Squash	Jalapeño	Jerusalem Artichoke (Topinambur)
Jicama	Kale	Kidney Beans	Kohlrabi
Leek	Legumes	Lentils	Lettuce
Lima Beans (Butter Beans)	Mangetout (Snap Peas)	Marrow (UK)/ Squash (US)	Mung Beans

Mushrooms (actually a fungus, not a plant)	Mustard Greens	Navy Beans	Nettles
New Zealand Spinach	Okra	Onion	Paprika
Parsley	Parsnip	Patty Pans	Peas
Peppers (biologically fruits, but taxed as vegetables)	Pinto Beans	Pumpkin	Quandong
Quinoa	Radicchio	Radish	Rhubarb
Root Vegetables	Runner Beans	Rutabaga	Salsify (Oyster Plant)
Scallion (Spring Onion UK/Green Onion US)	Shallot	Skirret	Soybeans
Spaghetti Squash	Spinach	Split Peas	Squashes
Sunchokes	Sweet Corn	Sweet Potato	Tabasco Pepper
Tat Soi	Tomato	Tubers	Turnip
Wasabi	Water Chestnut	Watercress	White Radish
Yam			

FRUITS

Açaí	Ackee	Apple
Apricot	Avocado	Banana
Bilberry	Blackberry	Blackcurrant
Black Sapote	Blood Orange	Blueberry
Boysenberry	Buddha's Hand (Fingered Citron)	Cantaloupe
Cherimoya (Custard Apple)	Cherry	Chico Fruit
Clementine	Cloudberry	Coconut
Crab Apples	Cranberry	Cucumber
Currant	Damson	Date
Dragon Fruit (Pitaya)	Durian	Elderberry
Feijoa	Fig	Goji Berry
Gooseberry	Grape	Grapefruit
Guava	Honeyberry	Honeydew
Huckleberry	Jabuticaba	Jackfruit
Jambul	Japanese Plum	Jostaberry
Jujube	Juniper Berry	Kiwano (Horned Melon)
Kiwifruit	Kumquat	Lemon
Lime	Longan	Loquat

Lychee	Mandarin	Mango
Mangosteen	Marionberry	Melon
Miracle Fruit	Mulberry	Nance
Nectarine	Olive	Orange
Papaya	Passionfruit	Peach
Pear	Persimmon	Pineapple
Pineberry	Plantain	Plum
Plumcot (Pluot)	Pomegranate	Pomelo
Prune (Dried Plum)	Purple Mangosteen	Quince
Raisin	Rambutan (Mamin Chino)	Raspberry
Redcurrant	Salak	Salal Berry
Salmonberry	Satsuma	Soursop
Star Apple	Star Fruit	Strawberry
Surinam Cherry	Tamarillo	Tamarind
Tangerine	Ugli Fruit	Watermelon
White Currant	White Sapote	Yuzu

WHOLE GRAINS

Amaranth	Barley	Brown rice
Buckwheat	Bulgur	Farro
Kamut	Maize	Millet
Oats	Quinoa	Red Rice
Rye	Spelt	Teff
Tricale	Wheat	Wild Rice

LOW GLYCEMIC (GI) FOODS[16]

Low-GI Foods (Under 55)	Medium-GI Foods (55–70)	High-GI Foods (Over 70)
Barley, Bulgar	Brown or Basmati Rice	Breakfast Cereals
Butter Beans and Peas	Couscous	Cookies
Milk	Honey	Instant Pasta
Most Fruits	Orange Juice	Pineapples and Melons
Non-Starchy Vegetables	Quick Oats	Russet Potatoes
Rolled or Steel-Cut Oats	Rye Bread	Short-Grain White Rice
Sweet Potatoes	Wholemeal Bread	White Bread

MY ANTI-INFLAMMATORY JOURNEY

There's an abundance of information out now regarding foods and inflammation. Of course, because I read everything I can find online about health and wellness, to me, it appears everywhere. When I started writing this book, I knew I would write something about it. It struck a note with me particularly after my doctor's comments 15 years ago regarding my chronic inflammation and cancer—although I knew the context was different. Nonetheless, I was hoping to create a simple list of "Eat this, don't eat that." The reality is there's not enough evidence to make it medically or scientifically viable yet, but there is a lot of compelling anecdotal evidence out there, including my own. (Yes, I'm comfortable that some folks will disagree with this.)

My personal experience is that I feel great sometimes and I feel lethargic and full other times, and I believe these feelings are related to the foods I've eaten. Many friends and coworkers agree, yet we can't support the cause and effect with science. In the past, I logged my food and still couldn't make direct connections. So, I continued my search.

My research brought me to the LEAP Diet (Lifestyle Eating And Performance), which addresses food-associated inflammatory conditions. Examples include arthritis, irritable bowel syndrome, diabetes, and ulcerative colitis. While I only have osteo-arthritis in my back and not these other conditions, I decided I would try it. This is where things got interesting, as there were numerous steps required **before** I tried my personalized LEAP diet. Stay tuned.

Simultaneously, I met with a friend, Cece Davis Gifford, who is a veteran nutritional consultant, registered dietician, and certified specialist in sport dietetics. My plan was to ask questions of her related to food and fitness and this book. Instead, we detoured, and she told me how her practice had evolved and that she was a Certified LEAP Therapist (CLT). It's a coincidence that these topics intersected with one person. I had known and trusted her for years, and she had helped me with cholesterol and low blood sugar issues in years past. It was then I decided to be my own test subject for the LEAP anti-inflammatory diet.

Here's an overview of the general 8+ week process:

Before the LEAP Diet begins

1. Complete the Initial Symptom Survey.
2. Get blood drawn and send to a lab to test for inflammatory reaction against 170 foods.
3. Share results with nutritionist after the lab identifies foods that are inflammatory for you.
4. Have the nutritionist design a personal LEAP elimination diet—orientation and Phase 1.

Beginning the LEAP Diet

5. Phase 1—Begin elimination diet; that is, eliminate all foods except those on the "approved" list. Log all food and drink into a food diary, and record symptoms, side-effects, and how you feel.
6. Meet with the nutritionist to review progress, including symptoms.
7. Phase 2—Add one new food per day for one week. Choose foods based on the nutritionist's suggestions.
8. Phase 3—Allow all foods from Phases 1 and 2, and add one new food a day for a week from a list of new options provided by the nutritionist.

9. Phase 4—Allow all foods from Phases 1, 2, and 3. Once again, you may add one new food a day for a week from the list of new options. Repeat.

10. Phase 5—Continue progression of adding new foods.

11. Wrap up—By this time, you've had food restrictions for at least two months, maybe more, depending on your symptoms.

The first step is to complete an Initial Symptom Survey, followed by a blood test. From this analysis, the nutritionist designs an elimination diet for a period of approximately five weeks. Sometimes, the process can take longer depending on the test results and experiences during the LEAP experience. The first week is the toughest because you eliminate all foods that are "Reactive," "Moderately Reactive," and above a specific marker of "Non-Reactive." After the first week, the nutritionist adds foods back into your diet based on the results of your Follow-Up Symptom Survey and discussion. Each week, acceptable foods are added back into one's diet.

LET THE GAMES BEGIN!

My blood was drawn and sent overnight to Oxford Biomedical Technologies Inc. in Florida. There, they tested my blood against 170 foods to identify whether any of them created inflammatory reactions. (By the way, this does *not* test for food allergies.) In two days, my nutritionist confirmed the receipt of the results, and she shared her advice with me.

My top inflammatory foods were identified as sugar, corn, and soy. OK, I thought, *"I can live without those,"* (forgetting that their byproducts are in <u>everything</u>). However, out of the 170 foods tested, I had inflammatory reactions to 125 of them, which meant there were only 45 safe foods. Things were going downhill fast. Some of the compounds that tested as inflammatory were identified in several of the acceptable foods, but those were eliminated, too. For example, solanine had a moderate reaction and it is in tomatoes, potatoes, peppers, eggplant, and paprika—even though the individual foods did not test negatively. Solanine is one reason these foods called "nightshades" get a bad rap.

With guidance from the nutritionist, I started my Phase 1 elimination diet. The first stage of eight days was difficult because I was limited to 20 foods. It threw a monkey wrench into my entire eating habits. On days three and four, I felt terrible. Apparently, the adjustment and detox were in full process. I was irritable and foggy headed. I had a headache for two and a half days. I was lethargic and didn't smile much. I didn't feel well overall, but I couldn't put my finger on it, except to acknowledge that I was warned this would happen. Within a few days, all of this would clear, and I would feel significantly better and more alert. I was getting into the groove of what I could eat and began to experiment mixing more foods in. The swelling in my hands went away, I was no longer bloated, and I felt trim. By the time I had my follow-up appointment, I was only missing the taste of coffee (I stopped drinking caffeine), tomatoes, onions, and fruit other than watermelon and cantaloupe.

Phase 1 confession: I have no kids at home and my husband was out of town. It made the process much easier, as I could focus on my nutritional needs only and not prepare multiple meals for multiple people and be tempted by what others might be eating.

Here's a list of my Phase 1 acceptable food list:

Proteins—Chicken, cod, sole, pork, pinto beans, kidney beans, and egg white

Grains—Millet, sweet potato

Vegetables—Butternut squash, green peas, bok choy

Fruits—Watermelon, cantaloupe, organic dates

Dairy—Goat milk and goat cheese

Nuts—Pistachio, flaxseed, and cashews

Flavor Enhancers—Salt, dill, rosemary, leeks, scallions, ginger, garlic, honey, coconut oil

When I kicked off Phase 2, I was excited that I was allowed to add one new food a day for seven days. I carefully selected my options. Coconut oil was the first to go in exchange for olive oil— to me there is no comparison. On day two, I was so grateful to have a mango, I savored half during breakfast and saved the other half for lunch. Each day I added a new food. I had 10 days under my belt and began experimenting more while cooking. I went out to eat once and reviewed the menu in advance to identify foods that were acceptable. I went to a small dinner party and asked the host for the menu in advance. I could eat some of the items she prepared and also brought my own food to share with the guests. Alcohol is not allowed, as it is inflammatory for everyone. This was tough because I'm a social drinker and they were making Manhattans (one of my favorites).

Here's a sample of what I added to my acceptable food list in Phase 2:

Protein—Shrimp

Grains—Cashew flour

Vegetables—Broccoli

Fruit—Mango and blueberries

Dairy—Goat milk and cheese (added here; allowed in Phase 1)

Nuts, Seeds, and Oils—Olive oil

Flavor Enhancers—Parsley and lime

Phase 3 continued the pattern of being able to add one new food per day. Finally, pasta! OK, it had to be made with chickpeas, and I still couldn't eat tomatoes … but I could make this work.

In addition, I talked with my nutritionist, Cece, who gave me suggestions of where to find specific foods in town and online. I could only find certain items online, like puffed brown rice to make in a sweet cereal bar recipe. Yet, gluten-free pasta was available in my local grocery stores including Walmart, Whole Foods, and Trader Joe's. I mentioned to Cece how difficult this would be for people who don't cook and eat out all the time. Her response is that they don't participate in the LEAP program, as that's a basic requirement. It made it much simpler that I liked to cook and experiment with different flavor combinations and new dishes.

I still considered myself a guinea pig in the experiment and it was expensive, but with a few savings, too. From the cost of the blood tests, appointments with nutritionists and special foods, it all added up. For me, though, it was worth it. Here are a few other thoughts:

- I saved quite a bit of money not going out to eat for lunch and dinner. Eventually, there were a few restaurants that could accommodate my restrictions, but I studied the menu in advance and even called a few restaurants to double check. And yes, many restaurants don't update their menus online, which created challenges. That's life!

- You can't bring others with you. Since foods are identified with your personal chemistry in mind, the limitations may not benefit others.

- It's inconvenient. It's far easier to prepare all your own food, but it requires more thought and planning. Furthermore, if you're cooking for others, it may prove to be even more challenging.

In the middle of Phase 3, some of the restrictions started to be no fun. I wanted to eat what I wanted when I wanted, yet I stuck to it. Other moments, I had momentum and felt disciplined and good about my progress. I was sleeping well, didn't wake up as tired and was feeling good during the day without relying on caffeine. I was hot more often, not quite hot flashes, but enough to take the sweater off and then back on (related?). I was no longer bloated or having bouts of digestive distress, except after my cheat day. Even though I usually had a snack mid-afternoon in the past, the snacks weren't always effective. During LEAP, I still had an afternoon lull, but even these were declining. And, in some way, the inconveniences were declining as well. I was integrating new foods and combinations into my diet and some of them would become permanent. However, I was still cautious about what the final phases of the elimination diet would bring and wondered what my eating habits would be after my experiment was over.

By week five, I was winding down in Phase 4. I was rounding the bend and getting excited about finishing Phase 5. I missed bread, crackers, avocado, chocolate, and salads. It was hard to find a bread with amaranth, millet, cashew, or oat flour. I missed my morning smoothies. But, I had gotten this far; I might as well continue, right?

Surprisingly, there were a few foods I didn't miss: dairy (cow), corn, soy, sugar, and beef. I was irritated because I was allowed to drink decaf coffee, but no longer had the taste for it. I missed my morning coffee ritual and instead drank hot water with ginger. I was following all of the rules. I also lost a few pounds, even though that wasn't the goal.

I learned there were foods and recipes that I could incorporate into my meal planning. I discovered my sweet tooth could be satisfied with dates, a "biscuit" made with cashew flour, or a homemade cereal bar made with puffed millet, cashew butter, honey, and coconut. In looking back, those foods had never been in my repertoire. By weeks four and five, I didn't feel hungry or deprived; I always found a food or created a dish to fit my palate.

I went out to eat occasionally and learned to check menus online in advance. However, I was predominantly planning and preparing my own meals and bringing lunches and snacks to work. Each week, I had to choose which one new food to try each day. It was like a present that I could select and savor. Most of the time it was fun making the selection— I'll take a pear over a grapefruit any day—but sometimes the choices were not nearly as enticing. Hmm … cranberries, sesame, walnuts, or black pepper today? Not appealing to me, but I wasn't suffering by any means. I think I didn't like being restricted and told what to do. My self-talk reminded me that this was my choice, not a requirement or punishment. Nevertheless, I really wanted a sandwich on bread with mustard and maybe avocado, too!

I finally got to Phase 5. Happy Day! By then, I had 18 new food additions, and I could choose one new food per day for a week, and then, I would be done. I chose yogurt—my first cow dairy in four weeks. I also had a session with the nutritionist to discuss maintenance—my maintenance (I felt a little bit like a car or motorcycle). I was a little nervous that I'd go on a food binge after the fifth week. It wouldn't have been out of hunger, but out of frustration, unfulfilled wants, and missing specific flavors, such as dark chocolate. (While I was on the LEAP diet, my brother shipped me six pints of my favorite Graeter's ice cream for my birthday. I never even had one bite!) By the end of Phase 5, my acceptable food list had grown to 63 options; not much, but it seemed like a buffet after the past month.

NOT ALL FUN AND GAMES

So, were there drawbacks? Sure. It was inconvenient for me and people around me. Others want to please and accommodate, and the restrictions are difficult to adhere to. Folks that I may normally share a glass of wine with felt a bit sorry for me as I held my glass of club soda. Conversely, I volunteered to be the designated driver, which reduced risk or saved us an Uber charge. Here are a few other considerations if you ever try this on your own.

SOCIAL

Where my social activities often centered around food and drink, I had to find alternatives or plan ahead. I don't eat out too often, but even I was constrained. I was quite dedicated, and it wasn't worth it to compromise my efforts. This also included invitations to friends' homes, which could be difficult. Sometimes, I ate before going out and brought my own food to activities. Even my husband was eating different foods than I was on most days and I was jealous, but persevered.

MEAL PLANNING AND SHOPPING

There's not much planning needed early when you're limited to 20 foods. However, over time, I learned to be more creative combining allowed foods and spices. My nutritionist gave me recipes and tips, and there's a helpful Pinterest site for people on LEAP diets. Fortunately, I like to cook and am willing to experiment, but folks who don't cook, or who eat out a lot—or those who travel—would have a difficult time with the LEAP program. Shopping became precise and my husband or I ran to the store a bit more often, as I ran out of an item or was allowed a new ingredient.

CELEBRATIONS AND DO-OVERS

When starting the LEAP diet, I didn't pay close attention to my calendar, which included an upcoming birthday. A big one that ended in "0." As the date got closer, I decided I would stay on the diet. Yet, in a conversation with a coworker, she brought up that others would ask, "What happened when you went off the diet?" Her comment was brilliant. Of course, I must go off the diet for my birthday in order to answer that question!

When I called Cece, she said I would get sick if I went off the diet and ate too many restricted foods. My gut (think stomach and intestines) was healing, and my system wouldn't be happy with the inflammatory foods. She specifically called it, "digestive distress" (code phrase for diarrhea). Not only that, once you go off, you must step back to the prior phase for three to four days without symptoms before you can resume where you were before the transgression. For me, that meant I had to go back to Phase 1.

For my birthday, my coworkers brought me chocolate cake after lunch, and I had more chocolate and other delicious foods at dinner. During my birthday dinner celebration with friends, I felt good because of the champagne, and had no physical repercussions. The day after was fine, too. Hah—I was going to be the exception! Until two days after the birthday celebration, when, let's just say I was wrong and Cece was right about the "digestive distress." I had a bloated, uncomfortable miserable day at home, and then humbly took steps back in the program to make up for my birthday celebration foods. At least I knew what would happen if I ate foods that weren't allowed.

TRAVEL

In Phase 4, I traveled out of town for a night. Since I was driving, I could bring quite a bit of food with me just in case. Overall, I lucked out at our hotel and the meeting luncheon buffet offered options I could eat, but I was glad I had brought my own snacks. It would be nearly impossible to travel during Phase 1 or 2 unless you were staying somewhere you can prepare your own meals. Furthermore, if you're traveling for fun, don't you want to enjoy the food and drink of the location you're visiting?

FAST FORWARD

After five months on the LEAP eating plan, I had my annual physical scheduled and since I was in overall good health, I didn't expect any new results. I had a nice surprise! I lost weight, my blood pressure was lower, my total cholesterol was lower, and my HDL was higher. I have the unique genetic combination of high total cholesterol and high HDL from working out. Because of this I get a warning from the doctor, but then receive praise because my ratio is so good. At my local gym, they tracked my measurements. My Body Mass Index (BMI) and fat percentage had significantly improved. I knew I felt better, saw the results on the scale, and had more energy. I had no specific goals when I started and was delighted with the end results.

Over six months, I narrowed my list of top foods to avoid to: sugar, corn, soy, wheat, beef, and cow dairy products (except Greek yogurt). I am now conscious of not eating or limiting grapes and wine, sunflower seeds, and nightshade plants, which are white potatoes, tomatoes, peppers, and eggplant. It sounds restrictive, yet I find that I can accommodate it with minimal effort. Of course, it's easier at home, yet I socialize now and eat out with little trouble.

In fairness, I had a fairly healthy lifestyle of good eating habits and exercise before I started my LEAP eating experiment. It would have been much more difficult if I had started this journey after eating lots of fast food, packaged and processed products, and restaurant food that was heavy with sugar, fat, and salt. These selections are common in my home state where we favor large portions and have high obesity to show for it. Also, those six months shed light on the amount of sugar and bread I consumed. I particularly like my baked goods and cookies, chocolate, crackers, and breads. I choose not to bake because I can't fight the temptation. I've found and developed some honey-based substitutes and dramatically reduced my interest in sugar while increasing my fruit intake. I am not against carbohydrates, in fact, it has been hard to give up the many grains I ate in the past, which I now know contain gluten. With the gluten-free restriction, I naturally eat less bread and crackers because they're not readily available. Finally, I was pleased with how many restaurants now have information about food allergies, offer gluten-free menus and selections, and/or were willing to accommodate my requests. I was committed to my eating program, but I wasn't going to be the friend and diner that ruined the event for everyone by being demanding. I worked to fit in and select without creating a scene, and I accomplished this.

There were social occasions when my food limitations bothered others more than me. This was especially true with alcohol. I have a new appreciation for people who have a variety of health requirements. There are social pressures everywhere … *"just one bite, just one drink."* I've learned not to create the shame and discomfort that type of cajoling may bring others. This realization is a real gift, and one that I certainly didn't expect while modifying my diet.

The word "diet" has such negative connotations. Let's remind ourselves that the word diet does *not* relate to limitations and restrictions. It relates to our **lifestyle** of eating snacks and meals. We hear of the benefits of a Mediterranean diet. This is the eating style of those who live in and around the Mediterranean Ocean. They don't have a list of do's and don'ts posted in their kitchen; it's simply a lifestyle based on foods available in the region. Yes, they're exceptional role models. We're lucky we can replicate their eating style because of the extensive availability of foods in the United States, and by doing so, may improve our own health. However, what we reach for in our refrigerators, what we purchase in our supermarkets, what we stock in our pantries, and what we order at restaurants is an illustration of our food and eating lifestyle. And, this was the real lesson I learned after changing my eating patterns over a six-month period. My lifestyle and choices changed over time. The process started out with difficult sacrifices, cravings, and physical side effects. But, as I went further into the program, I had more energy; and my experiment didn't have a definite end date as I had expected because it is not a diet in the American use of the term; it is merely a new and revised lifestyle.

Review Inquiry

Hey, it's Jane Mudgett here.

I hope you've enjoyed the book, finding it both useful and fun. I have a favor to ask you.

Would you consider giving it a rating on Amazon (or wherever you bought the book)? Online book stores are more likely to promote a book when they feel good about its content, and reader reviews are a great barometer for a book's quality.

So please go to **Amazon.com** (or wherever you bought the book), search for my name and the book title, and leave a review. If someone gave you a copy of my book, then leave a review on Amazon, and maybe consider adding a picture of you holding the book - that increases the likelihood your review will be accepted!

Many thanks in advance,

JANE MUDGETT

Will You Share the Love?

GET THIS BOOK FOR A FRIEND, ASSOCIATE, OR FAMILY MEMBER!

If you have found this book valuable and know others who would find it useful, consider buying them a copy as a gift. Special bulk discounts are available if you would like your whole team or organization to benefit from reading this. Just contact me at **jane@5-alive.com** or **https://exceptionalleaderslab.com/janemudgett/**.

Would You Like Jane Mudgett to Speak to Your Organization?

BOOK JANE MUDGETT NOW!

Jane Mudgett accepts a limited number of speaking, coaching, and training engagements each year. To learn how you can bring her message to your organization, call or email:

Exceptional Leaders Lab at 918-779-7744,
melissa@exceptionalleaderslab.com,
or **jane@5-alive.com.**

ENDNOTES

1. Frost, Robert, The Road Not Taken: A Selection of Robert Frost's Poems, (New York: Henry Holt and Company, 1971), 270.

2. Kiplinger, Knight, "The Invisible Rich," Kiplinger.com, October 1, 2006, https://www.kiplinger.com/article/saving/T047-C014-S002-the-invisible-rich.html.

3. "Harnessing the Power of the Purse," Center for Talent Innovation, 2014, https://www.talentinnovation.org/_private/assets/HarnessingThePowerOfThePurse_Infographic-CTI.pdf.

4. Burton, Robyn, and Nick Sheron, "No level of alcohol consumption improves health," The Lancet 392, no. 10152 (2018): 987-988.

5. Davis, Adelle, Let's Eat Right To Keep Fit, (New York: Signet, 1954).

6. "30 Foods High in Sodium and What to Eat Instead," Healthline, accessed October, 28, 2019. https://www.healthline.com/nutrition/foods-high-in-sodium.

7. Julia Child, Mastering the Art of French Cooking, Volume 2 (New York: Knopf, 1970), 55.

8. Wallis, Claudia, "The Messy Facts about Diet and Inflammation," Scientific American 318, no. 1 (2018): 22-22, doi:10.1038/scientificamerican0118-22.

9. "Heart Disease Maps and Data Sources," State of Childhood Obesity: Helping All Children Grow Up Healthy, Accessed October 7, 2019, https://www.cdc.gov/heartdisease/maps_data.htm.

10. "Physical Activity Guidelines," Office of Disease Prevention and Health Promotion, Accessed February 7, 2019, https://health.gov/our-work/physical-activity.

11. Dalai Lama, Desmond Tutu, and Douglas Carlton Abrams, The Book of Joy: Lasting happiness in a changing world, (New York: Penguin, 2016).

12. Harmon, Katherine, "Social Ties Boost Survival by 50 Percent," Scientific American, July 28, 2010, https://www.scientificamerican.com/article/relationships-boost-survival/.

13. https://www.squaresail.com/ileshtpy.html

14. Hartwell-Walker, Marie, "The Benefits of Play" Psych Central. Accessed October 25, 2019, https://psychcentral.com/lib/the-benefits-of-play/.

15. Gordon, Neil F., Richard D. Salmon, Brenda S. Wright, George C. Faircloth, Kevin S. Reid, and Terri L. Gordon, "Clinical Effectiveness of Lifestyle Health Coaching: Case Study of an Evidence-Based Program," American Journal of Lifestyle Medicine 11, no. 2 (2017): 153–166. https://www.ncbi.nlm.nih.gov/pmc/articles/PMC6125027/.

16. Burgess, Lana, "What are the best low-glycemic foods?" Medical News Today. Accessed February 14, 2020. https://www.medicalnewstoday.com/articles/324871.php#how-the-scale-works

ABOUT THE AUTHOR

Do you have the funds for your current and future lifestyle? Do you have a Circle of Trust? Do you feel healthy and energetic? Do you have interests outside of work that make you smile?

Jane Mudgett takes living seriously – sort of. She has an extensive love and zest for travel and has visited all of the United States and all seven continents. Her favorite place is always her last trip. As a 15+ year cancer survivor, her key values are having new experiences and living her life to the fullest.

She is a deeply experienced leader, coach, and trainer. She's a partner at Exceptional Leaders Lab. Jane specializes in enhancing lifestyle and longevity for individuals and employees through her proprietary program, 5 Alive. The program is focused on positive behaviors in the five key areas of Finance, Food, Fitness, Fun, and Friends. Over the last 30 years, Jane has facilitated leadership training in the automotive, energy, and financial industries. She is an active community volunteer and regularly presents programs on long-term health and wellness, estate planning, empowering women, financial management, and leadership.

Jane's personal motto is that, "It's better to have 10 new experiences, than the same experience 10 times."

Jane lives in Tulsa, OK with her husband.

Jane Mudgett can be reached at: **jane@5-alive.com** and
https://www.5-alive.com

Made in the USA
Columbia, SC
17 March 2020